RESERVE OFFICERS TRAINING CORPS

Campus Pathways to Service Commissions

by

Col. Robert F. Collins
US Army (ret.)

THE ROSEN PUBLISHING GROUP

New York

Published in 1986 by The Rosen Publishing Group, Inc.
29 East 21st Street, New York City, New York 10010

First Edition
Copyright 1986 by Robert F. Collins

Library of Congress Cataloging-in-Publication Data

Collins, Robert F., 1938–
    Reserve Officers Training Corps.

    Includes index.
    1. United States. Army. Reserve Officers'
Training Corps.   I. Title.
U428.5.C55   1986   355.2′232   86–13744
ISBN 0-8239-0695-7

Manufactured in the United States of America

To the over one million young men and women who have been commissioned through ROTC and who have served their nation with courage, honor, integrity, and devotion.

Acknowledgments

The author wishes to acknowledge the assistance provided by the representatives of the Army, Navy, and Air Force, who were extremely helpful in giving their opinions and providing source material. Much of the material in the book was drawn directly from service publications. Particular mention must be made of the assistance rendered by Army Major Larry Olson, who devoted personal time to assisting me by providing current information and contacts in the other services. Brigadier General USAF (ret.) Monro MacCloskey should also receive special recognition for having written the first comprehensive book about the ROTC programs more than twenty years ago. I have drawn freely from his excellent work. Errors in the book, of course, are mine.

About the Author

Robert F. Collins is a recently retired officer who served more than twenty-five years in the US Army. He enlisted in the Army in 1960, graduated from Officer's Candidate School in 1962, and achieved the rank of Colonel before his retirement in 1985. Col. Collins was in the Military Intelligence branch and served tours of duty in Korea, Vietnam, Germany, and the United States. He is a Soviet Foreign Area Officer with extensive travel in Eastern Europe and the Soviet Union. He taught US National Security Policy at the US Army's Command and General Staff College for five years and was a Professor of Military Science for two years. His decorations include the Army Commendation Medal, the Meritorious Service Medal, the Bronze Star, and the Legion of Merit. He was one of the leading voices in the United States military on the importance of ROTC, and he has written extensively on the subject.

Contents

Introduction

The Reserve Officers Training Corps (ROTC) program is the single greatest supplier of officers to the Armed Forces today, for both active and reserve duty. In this sense, the program might more accurately be called the Officer Training Program rather than the Reserve Officers' Training Program. Senior ROTC programs are offered at over one thousand colleges and universities throughout the United States, Guam, and Puerto Rico. The Departments of the Army, Navy, and Air Force administer their own programs according to their own special needs, objectives, and foreseeable requirements. The Marine Corps does not have a separate program, but obtains regular and reserve officers from the Navy ROTC program. In some instances, all three services offer ROTC programs on the same campus; however, the programs are independent.

The ROTC program has experienced many ups and downs since its inception more than one hundred fifty years ago. Today it is a thriving program with a combined total of more than 200,000 young men and women enrolled in all three services. Both the civilian and military leadership of the United States realize the importance and value of the ROTC program to the security of the nation. ROTC provides the future leaders of the US military forces. ROTC provides the military leadership with a constant infusion of well-educated, idealistic, questioning, responsible young men and women college graduates that represent all sectors of society.

The purpose of this book is to present in one volume information on the ROTC programs of all three services to assist the young man or woman considering entering the program after high school or while already in university or college. Entering the ROTC program does not mean you have to serve a twenty-year career in the military; in fact, you have several options regarding active duty or reserve duty and length of commitment.

The first three chapters deal with the advantages and career benefits of the ROTC program, today's professional officer, and a brief historical background of the program. Chapters IV through VI contain specifics on the ROTC programs of the Army, Air Force, Navy, and Marine Corps. Organization and administration are examined; entrance criteria, selection procedures, and scholarships available to high school and college students are explained; pay, allowances, obligations, and benefits are discussed; education and training including summer training are detailed; special programs of each service are reviewed, and related campus activities are highlighted. The conclusion contains additional considerations relating to the ROTC programs. The appendix lists colleges and universities with established ROTC programs as well as sources of additional information. A current table of pay and allowances is included, as well as insignia of the armed forces and ROTC production figures.

This book is designed as a guide for the young man or woman considering ROTC and a service career, as well as a guide for parents, high school and college counselors, and job opportunity specialists. Entering the ROTC program does not obligate the person to a career in the military; most people who enter the program do not serve a twenty-year career in the military. All career choices should be examined carefully before decisions are made; this book should help students and parents to better understand their options.

RESERVE OFFICERS TRAINING CORPS

Chapter **I**

ROTC Advantages for the Student

The requirements for military officers for all the services cannot be filled by the service academies alone. With the elimination of the draft in the early 1970s, the services were forced to develop new programs and expand existing programs to attract the required numbers of both enlisted and officer personnel. National attitudes toward military service and projected decreasing numbers of available manpower indicate that fulfilling manpower goals in the late 1980s and the 1990s will be difficult for the armed forces. Consequently, they will probably continue to offer lucrative inducements to prospective students to enter the ROTC programs.

Currently, all services offer four-year scholarships to students, which pay for tuition, books, related educational expenses, lab fees, and travel expenses to the host institution. In addition, the scholarship cadets as well as contracted nonscholarship cadets receive a stipend of $100 a month up to ten months each school year. Competition is extremely keen for the four-year scholarships. Candidates are judged on grade point average, high school activities, community activities, College Board scores, academic interests, and ability to present themselves favorably before an interview board composed of military officers. All services also offer limited numbers of three- and two-year scholarships. Details on service scholarships are given in the chapters dealing with the individual services.

The ROTC program is attractive in many other ways. Many enrollees are motivated by patriotism and a desire to serve their country. That is one of the intangible benefits of military service along with opportunities to travel, to receive many additional years of schooling, to work with different kinds of people in many different situations, and to have a job that is secured by law.

ROTC is taken in colleges and universities in the same manner as other elective courses. A student does not major in ROTC or Military Affairs; rather, the student takes ROTC classes once or twice a week while pursuing his or her own choice of academic disciplines. All services need officers with highly technical scientific/engineering skills, and the majority of scholarships are awarded in the technical, engineering, and science areas. However, scholarships are also available in political science, the humanities, languages, etc. The ROTC training is different in detail within each service program, but all programs include instruction on communication, management, and leadership skills as well as subjects best called general officership. Emphasis is placed on both theoretical and practical training in leadership and executive techniques that will develop the student's potential to the maximum, and this training is an invaluable asset in any military or civilian career. Details on the services' curricula are given in Chapters IV through VI.

ROTC units on college and university campuses are staffed by active-duty personnel from the respective services. The Professor of Military Science (Army) and Professor of Air Science (Air Force) are either full colonels or lieutenant colonels; the Professor of Naval Science (Navy–Marine Corps) is either a captain or commander in the Navy and a colonel in the Marines. These military professors are members in full standing of the college faculty. They and their staffs are in close contact with their students. They not only provide instruction but also counseling and guidance on both personal and academic matters. What are some of the inducements offered by the federal government? Since they vary depending on the service, they are treated separately.

In the Army

ROTC graduates who successfully complete the Army ROTC program and graduate from a six-week summer advanced camp, which is usually attended between the junior and senior years, are commissioned in the US Army as Second Lieutenants. The majority of the new lieutenants are commissioned at the same time they receive their diploma from the university or college. Most of the new officers enter on active duty for a period of four years, although provisions are in effect for ROTC graduates to enter on reserve duty. ROTC graduates, upon being commissioned, receive a uniform allowance. ROTC officers receive the same pay, allowances, and fringe benefits as all other commissioned officers from the United States Military Academy at West Point or other special programs. Current tables of pay and allowances are given in the Appendix.

Academic credit is given for Army ROTC courses at colleges and universities. Complete uniforms and the textbooks required are furnished at government expense. ROTC is usually a four-year program, and third- and fourth-year students receive a $100 a month stipend up to $1,000 a year. Students receive $700 for attending a six-week advanced camp between their junior and senior years, as well as travel expenses to and from the camp.

The army offers many other opportunities for cadets in the ROTC program, including opportunities to attend such Army schools as flight training, airborne school, Ranger school, and a nurse summer training program in lieu of advanced camp. The Army also has a Simultaneous Membership Program (SMP), which permits students to serve as officer trainees in the Army National Guard or Army Reserve while enrolled as ROTC cadets. SMP members receive drill pay for their National Guard or Army Reserve duties as well as the normal $100 monthly stipend from ROTC. The army also offers the Technological Enrichment Program (TEP). This is a highly competitive program developed for newly commissioned officers to attend graduate school in a high-tech discipline. It is a specialized program that accepts only thirty officers each year nationwide. The Army, like the other services, also offers programs for select individuals to continue their education after completing the undergraduate degree.

In the Air Force

Two routes to an Air Force commission are available to college students in the Air Force ROTC program. Entering students may enroll in the four-year program, and students with at least two academic years remaining in college may apply for the two-year program. Air Force ROTC courses normally are taken for academic credit as part of a student's electives. The program offers a variety of extra activities to its cadets; among them are Flight Instruction Program (FIP), advanced training program, base visits, and airborne training. ROTC pilot candidates not yet certified as private pilots participate in the Flight Instruction Program, which is conducted during the last twenty-four months of ROTC and is at Air Force expense. Flying lessons are taken at a Federal Aviation Administration–approved civilian flying school. Selected cadets may have the opportunity to go to active Air Force bases for a two- or three-week period during the summer following their junior year. Cadets receive pay and allowances authorized by current directives at the time of advanced training attendance. Air Force

ROTC cadets may have the opportunity to visit Air Force bases. These trips usually are made on weekends or scheduled to coincide with school vacation periods. Cadets may be flown by military aircraft to an Air Force base, where they receive facility tours and mission briefings and inspect aircraft and other technical equipment. Selected cadets may attend airborne training as an extracurricular activity. On completion of the airborne school, Air Force ROTC cadets may wear the Army "jump wings."

Air Force ROTC scholarships are available to qualified applicants in both the four- and two-year programs. Each scholarship provides full tuition, laboratory and incidental fees, and full reimbursement for curriculum-required textbooks. Additionally, scholarship cadets receive a nontaxable subsistence allowance each month of $100 during the school year while on a scholarship status. Other scholarship opportunities exist on a competitive basis for students already enrolled in college. An Air Force Pre-Health Professions Scholarship program (Pre-HPSP) in selected medical areas is offered to encourage students to earn commissions through Air Force ROTC and go on to acquire doctorates in health care fields. The Air Force pays for the remaining health profession schooling. Student nurses pursuing at least a baccalaureate degree at a National League of Nursing–accredited school of nursing or certain state-approved schools of nursing are eligible to enroll in either the four-year or two-year Air Force ROTC program. They may also compete for two-year scholarships that will help finance the last two years of college.

Cadets in the last two years of the Air Force ROTC program may travel free on military aircraft on a space-available basis, and cadets in the Flight Instruction Program receive up to thirteen hours of free flight training while in school.

In the Navy

The Navy–Marine Corps ROTC program is similar in many respects to the other service programs. The Navy program offers both four-year and two-year scholarships. Like the Air Force, the Navy encourages its ROTC cadets to pursue degrees in engineering and the sciences. The four-year scholarships are awarded annually on a competitive basis. The scholarships cover full tuition, lab fees, uniforms, related academic costs, and $100 per month tax free, up to ten months per academic year. The Navy two-year ROTC scholarships provide tuition, fees, books, and uniforms for two academic

International relations on a summer cruise.

years with a $100 stipend per month for up to ten months per academic year. When accepted as a two-year scholarship winner, the student attends the six-week Naval Science Institute course at New-port, Rhode Island, during the summer between his or her sopho-more and junior years. The student studies the subjects covered in the freshman and sophomore years in the Navy ROTC curriculum. The student is reimbursed for travel expenses to and from Newport and also receives pay during the six-week period.

The Navy also offers a nonsubsidized ROTC Navy-Marine Corps program. These Naval ROTC cadets, called College Program stu-dents, enter either the four-year or two-year program, take the same courses, wear the same type of uniform, and graduate with their contemporaries, but attend college at their own expense. They take all the naval science courses and upon successful completion and graduation are commissioned to serve on active duty for three years. College Program students also receive uniforms and all books required for naval science courses. During the junior and senior years, they also receive $100 per month for a maximum of ten months each academic year. They attend a summer training period between the junior and senior academic years.

Marine Corps midshipmen participate in the same basic program as Navy midshipmen for the first two years. This includes a summer session of military training. Beginning with the junior year, they are taught Marine Corps-oriented courses and are counseled on the duties and opportunities of Marine Corps officers. Marine Corps officers, like Navy officers, can be selected for flight training at Naval Air Station, Pensacola, Florida.

Successful completion of all the service ROTC programs leads to commissioning as an officer in the Army, Navy, Air Force, or Marines.

Chapter II

Today's Professional Officer

The officer in today's armed forces must understand the unique role that the military plays in the American form of government. It is a role that has been shaped by experience, tradition, and the unique American values of individual worth and personal freedom. The tradition of soldiery has not developed in the United States: Indeed, from the very beginning of the American national experience there has been general agreement that a large standing army was neither desired nor required. This belief was based on many circumstances. Starting with the colonial experience, with hope for the future and tremendous optimism, the early American settlers were strongly independent and convinced that they were able to protect themselves. One of the reasons they had left Europe was to escape militarized, regimented, authoritarian societies; the American experience encouraged self-reliance, with security concerns best handled by oneself and one's immediate neighbors. It is only since the end of World War II that Americans have come to realize that there is a valid requirement to have relatively large professional armed forces not only in place but also prepared to fight if necessary on short notice.

The United States has been blessed by its location from a security standpoint. Until the beginning of the twentieth century it was relatively invulnerable to attack by foreign powers. Flanked by oceans on both east and west and having friendly neighbors on north and south, the United States developed its traditions and way of looking at the rest of the world in a secure, relatively isolated manner. An abundance of natural resources, temperate climate, and productive agricultural lands further promoted its independence and self-reliance. The United States did not play a world role until this century, and no large standing military force was required to protect it from invaders, keep the sea lanes open, or guarantee the freedom of the air. Conflicts were local and usually of short duration. When faced with an emergency, the American people rallied to the call for arms, fought bravely, and attempted to resolve the conflict quickly. Military leaders have emerged in time of crisis and received honor and adulation for their deeds, but the American people have always insisted that the citizen army be disbanded as soon as the crisis was over.

Americans have always been sensitive to the dangers of too strong a military influence on government. Indeed, one of the bedrock tenets of our democracy, guaranteed by the Constitution, is the civilian control of the military. It is an inviolable rule that the military only carries out policy; the military cannot make government policy. The role of the military leader is to advise civilian decision-makers and then implement their decisions. Viewing eighteenth- and nineteenth-century Europe and military takeovers by Cromwell, Frederick the Great, and Napoleon reinforced the American idea of a small military to be expanded with citizens if emergencies arose. A small professional force would be able to carry out most missions requiring military force, and if necessary, American fighting troops could be mobilized for large-scale conflicts. This idea worked well for the United States until this century, but now circumstances and the world situation have altered drastically.

The United States today is the acknowledged leader of the free world; the United States has global responsibilities and global obligations. The United States does not covet territory, and it is not a militaristic nation, but it must have an adequate standing military force to protect its own interests and the interests of the other democratic nations as well. Our boundaries, so secure for hundreds of years, are now vulnerable to attack from both the air and the sea. Our frontiers now extend to the Far East, to Africa, Europe, and Asia, the Caribbean, and the Indian subcontinent. The world has grown much smaller, thanks to technology and human progress. Events that occur in distant countries now have repercussions that directly affect the United States economically, militarily, and politically. It is no longer valid to view the world as divided into communist and capitalist camps; other actors play important regional roles, and the balance of power is constantly shifting. Military officers today not only must be technically and tactically proficient in their fighting skills; they must also have a grounding in international relations and be sensitive to political, economic, and social changes around the world.

A Marine Corps midshipman.

The professional career officer has an important role in the American way of life. He has dedicated his life to the service of his country. Under extreme circumstances he is willing to place his life on the line for the defense of the nation. His devotion to duty carries a moral as well as a professional obligation. The standards of conduct for the professional officer are well defined and apply both on and off duty. It is often said that serving in the armed forces is a twenty-four-hour-a-day job. The officer is expected to set an example and meet all obligations, both personal and private, in a professional manner. The best interests of the country come before any personal considerations. He accepts his commission voluntarily. He serves at the order of and under the authority of the President of the United States. In taking his oath of office, he swears to "support and defend the Constitution of the United States against all enemies, foreign or domestic."

The military profession is dedicated to service, and officers serve with honor. The code of honor system must be strictly observed, whether as an ROTC cadet, a military cadet or midshipman at the service academies, or on active duty. The professional officer is expected not to quibble, hedge, or offer excuses, but to carry out his duties to the best of his ability once decisions are made. The officer is encouraged to make reasoned judgments and provide his advice to his superiors before decisions are made. Once a decision is made, the officer is expected to support and carry it out as best he can. An officer's word and signature are his bond; he will never knowingly lie, cheat, or steal. He will never disregard or slack off on the military mission for personal gain. An officer keeps his promises and meets his financial obligations. His moral character, his integrity, his courage, and his devotion to duty are above reproach.

During most of the history of this country, the military has been relatively isolated from the civilian community. Military personnel usually were stationed in isolated posts, were serving in foreign countries, or perhaps were stationed in ships at sea. There was no draft until this century, and not all sections of the public were fully represented in the military. As a result, the public at large knew very little about military customs and traditions, and the military in turn knew very little about public concerns and perspectives. The situation is quite different today. There are close and continuing contacts between military people and civilians at innumerable levels. The media—newspapers, TV, radio, and movies—provide extensive coverage of military operations, research and development, budgets, training, educational requirements, etc. In our democratic form of government, the people have a constitutional right to be informed of governmental activities—government in the sunshine. Military undertakings, if they are to be successful, must have the support of the people. Today's professional officer must understand that America's armed forces are indeed a people's armed forces, and that he serves the American people as a whole and not any special-interest groups. We learned many lessons from the Vietnam war, but the most important was that no war can be successfully prosecuted without the consent and active support of the US public.

The professional officer must accept the responsibilities of American citizenship to the degree that they are compatible with his military duties. Since his professional responsibilities require that he be nonpartisan in his actions, he cannot be publicly committed to one political party or faction as far as his official duties are concerned. He cannot use his official position as leader, manager, or supervisor to try to influence his subordinates in a particular political direction. Military officers are the executors of policy; the makers of policy are the duly elected *civilian* leaders and representatives of the people. That does not mean, however, that the professional officer should be uninterested in or uninformed about politics. The professional officer may not hold elective office while on active duty, but he is encouraged to vote and to participate in the political process. Even when the officer is stationed outside the United States, he is provided with information on both local and national elections so that he can make an informed vote. Voting is an obligation, a responsibility, and a privilege for all American citizens.

The professional officer is encouraged to participate in community activities and voluntary associations both on and off the military installation. Today, more than at any time in the past, a large percentage of military officers is likely to be living in civilian communities. More officers are working in civilian industries, attending civilian universities to obtain advanced degrees, and working in diversified areas away from strictly military duties.

ROTC officers and cadets are encouraged to participate in both university and community activities. The ROTC activity on campus does not operate in isolation; rather, it operates as an integral part of university activities and functions. The officers in the ROTC unit are representatives and spokesmen for their respective services. The cadets or midshipmen get involved in fund-raising events, current events presentations, university color guards, military equipment displays, community sporting events, and so on to publicize and promote the ROTC programs. These efforts to inform the public about military activities and the officer's participation in religious, civic, educational, recreational, and community improvement organizations are good for the military and good for the public. They allow the officer to gain an appreciation of the civilian point of view, and they go a long way to insure that the civilian community understands the military point of view. That is a good basis for effective civilian-military relations.

The professional officer today and tomorrow will face unique challenges: how to operate in an environment in which technology advances almost daily and military adversaries have the potential to destroy life. These challenges will be all the more difficult because basically it is against the American character to prepare for a future war. We believe that conflicts can and should be resolved by discussion and reason, with force used only as a last resort. We believe in the basic good of humanity and generally that our form of government and way of life are the best. We believe that government should serve the people and not vice versa. These are noble ideas, but we must remember that they are not shared by all governments around the world. Our world view works against programs to keep the military fully prepared on an immediate basis to respond to overt military attacks. The American tradition and ethic demand that the US can never be an aggressor nation, can never attack first, must conduct warfare in a honorable manner, must be threatened significantly before resorting to violence. The US public must be kept informed of how the war is being conducted and must be able to see a successful short conclusion to the conflict. These imperatives make service in the armed forces challenging and difficult. However, the main point about these conditions is that they are a genuine expression of the American character, and the military must operate within the bounds of the public's authority and approval.

Today's professional officers must possess more technical skills than officers in the past have been required to possess. All the services will have continuing demands for officers who possess engineering, scientific, computer, research, and technical skills. The armed forces will be at the forefront of exploring applications of the newest technologies in space, at sea, and on land. The operation of our complicated weapons systems and their backup and supporting units requires officers of a high level of technical knowledge and skill. The tremendous research and development effort of the armed forces also requires highly trained technicians. Some technicians are pure scientists interested in the development of fundamental disciplines. Some military technicians have the specific task of understanding scientific developments and relating them to the needs and missions of each service. The armed forces operate a great number of laboratories and facilities where the officers work, frequently with civilian experts, on the development of military technology.

To perform its essential function in national defense, each service must have highly qualified, well-educated, dedicated officers capable of executing the multitude of tasks necessary to readiness and to planning and preparing for the future. Probably many ROTC cadets who are in college qualifying for a service career will one day take on tasks that do not now exist and cannot even be imagined. The services require officers who are intelligent, resourceful, and visionary and who possess the necessary academic and technical credentials. However, as important as technical skills and expertise are, the main emphasis in all services is on leadership skills. Being an officer means that your first responsibility is to manage, supervise, and lead the men and women who work for you. Military leadership encompasses two major responsibilities: to accomplish the military mission, and to look out for the well-being of the people entrusted to your care. However, there are unique considerations in military leadership as compared to leadership in business, industry, or academic pursuits. No other profession makes demands on its members as does the military in wartime. In extreme circumstances, the military officer is called upon to assume responsibility for guarding the nation and, if necessary, fighting and making the ultimate sacrifice to preserve its way of life and its ideals—freedom, justice, and human dignity. In time of peace people are often motivated by personal gain and by survival and security needs. In time of war, however, the military officer must be able to inspire his or her people to sacrifice self-interest—possibly to sacrifice their lives—to carry out missions for the greater good of the service and the country. Leadership can be learned, and ROTC starts the lifelong process of learning those skills.

Specific skills of problem-solving, decision-making, planning, goal-setting, communicating, coordinating, supervising, evaluating, motivating, teaching, and counseling are required of military officers in all services. Today's professional officer cannot be effective and do his job properly if he is not people-oriented. The days of strict authoritarianism and unthinking obedience to all decisions are long gone, if in fact they ever existed at all. Today's military members are encouraged to think for themselves and to participate in the decision-making process. The American character does not allow a military whose members are mere automatons blindly following orders in a rigid structured system such as that of the Soviet Union. American military members contribute their thought and experience for the most efficient operation of their unit. Military officers should encourage the expression of and benefit from the opinions of their subordinates.

Today's professional officers must be prepared to operate effectively anywhere along the spectrum of conflict. That could range from limited unconventional war or combating terrorism to general nuclear war. The US policy in the nuclear age is one of deterrence. US armed forces must be strong enough to make all potential adversaries realize that the benefits gained from aggression against the United States or its allies will not be worth the risks involved. Potential adversaries must also be convinced of the United States' will to protect its interests. The likelihood of all-out nuclear war is very low in the foreseeable future; leaders of both the US and the Soviet Union realize that nuclear war has the potential to destroy life on earth. Still, the possibility exists of an unauthorized or accidental firing of a nuclear weapon or even a madman's choice to use a nuclear weapon. Having to cope with such a large range of possibilities imposes difficult burdens on the armed forces. The highest probability of conflict in the near future is low-level insurgencies and terrorist action in areas far distant from the United States. Today's military officer is forced to prepare for the possibility of military operations in Europe, Africa, Latin America, the Far East, and the Persian Gulf area. Tomorrow the officer will have to be flexible, able to respond on short notice, have the ability to work in any environment, be able to plan quickly and change plans as the situation demands, and be well versed in foreign cultures. It will be a difficult and professionally rewarding challenge.

Much has been written about the character of the US military. Today's all-volunteer force is necessarily different in many ways from a force depending on the draft for its manpower. The draft was discontinued in the US in the early 1970s. There are ongoing arguments as to whether it will be necessary to reinstate the draft to meet manpower requirements in the 1990s and beyond. Constantly changing attitudes toward military service and a decreasing manpower pool to draw from in the next ten years probably mean that the armed forces will have to increase recruiting efforts to meet goals. ROTC will be called upon to furnish at least 75 percent of all officers entering active duty each year. So, in a sense, the character of ROTC classes around the nation will be partly reflected as the character of the military.

The military constituency is drawn from the society it defends, and society as a whole has certain perceived images about the military. Society in a special sense looks to the military as possessing some of its most precious values. Moral integrity is synonymous with military officership.

To give but one example, consider the question of cheating in the universities. Cheating, according to most polls, is generally accepted by the public, and most people have developed a noncondemning attitude toward cheating by the age of ten. What is the public reaction to the latest report of cheating at a university? Generally speaking, there is little reaction, the public believing that cheating at a university is common. What is the public reaction to reports of cheating at a military academy? The story receives widespread media attention, committees are appointed to investigate the circumstances, immediate changes are called for, supervisory personnel are usually replaced. Somehow we feel that such things are just not supposed to happen at military academies. The point is that the public perceives moral integrity as such an essential part of military service that any hint of cheating or dishonesty must be quickly and completely examined and remedial measures taken if required.

Entrusting the security of the country to the military demands that the military demonstrate those values that are precious to the society. Public expectations of military officers' performance of duty go far beyond military knowledge and technical proficiency; the public expects military officers to exhibit loyalty, patriotism, obedience, selflessness, and above all, integrity. The profession itself is viewed as noble because it involves protecting the values that US citizens cherish most highly. Military officers must be aware of and comply with the public's expectations.

By being educated at civilian colleges and universities, ROTC students enjoy all the advantages of higher education while receiving the professional instruction and training of the ROTC program. In the process, ROTC students are exposed to the changes within our social structure. They can draw on sources for education in other professions that are closely allied to a military career. Having successfully completed their education and training, ROTC graduates are commissioned as full-time regular officers or professional reserve officers. As such, they continue the integration process of civilian and military leadership so essential to the future welfare of our nation.

Chapter **III**

Historical Background of the ROTC Program

The Reserve Officers Training Corps is a historic institution in the United States, marked by a proud tradition, that has continually been modified to meet the changing professional requirements of national defense. Particularly in this century, the US government has had to rely increasingly on the graduates of civilian colleges and universities to expand its Officer Corps quickly in time of war. ROTC was initially conceived to provide well-educated men from different parts of the society to serve in the state militia forces or for short periods in the federal military force. In its initial stages, ROTC was based on the concept of training reserve officers for a citizen army.

As was discussed in Chapter II, the concept of a citizen army responding as required to emergencies was derived from our colonial experiences. In 1792 it was written into law that a state militia system be established. Under the law, all free, white, male citizens between the ages of eighteen and forty-five years were liable for military service. Only Congress could mobilize and induct the citizen soldier into federal service, but the type and extent of training and discipline were the responsibility of the local commander.

The states then had the responsibility to provide trained officers for the militia. The first noncareer military college, the forerunner of ROTC, was established in Vermont in 1819 by Captain Alden Partridge, a former superintendent of the United States Military Academy at West Point. It was called the American Literary, Scientific and Military Academy, but in 1834 its name was changed to Norwich University. The mission of the academy was to train officers for the military who would be "identified in views, in feeling, in interests, with the great body of the community." Note that even with the passage of over 150 years, the mission of ROTC remains generally the same today—to provide trained officers to the military who represent the society they serve.

16

As early as 1824 the Army detailed a regular officer to instruct students in military theory and tactics at St. John's College in Annapolis. In the South, military colleges were founded along the lines of Norwich. They included Virginia Military Institute in 1839 and The Citadel in 1842. Military instructors were sent in 1840 to the University of Tennessee, one of the oldest of land-grant schools. Other military schools were established before the Civil War, as a result of Southern military tradition and because it was considered that discipline and self-restraint could best be taught by military training. These schools had little formal relationship with or direction from the state militia system, although many of their graduates became members of state military organizations.

When the Civil War broke out, the Northern forces encountered a great shortage of professional officers. Only 684 West Point graduates were in the Regular Army. The total officer strength was 1,098, but more than 300 officers resigned their commissions and served with the Confederacy. The rest served with Regular Army units, leaving the mobilized divisions of state troops to officers appointed by the governors. Most of these were nonprofessionals, although a few were Regular Army officers who had resigned their commissions. In the South the capability of the nonprofessional officers was enhanced by the training many of them had received in private and state military schools. The Citadel furnished 173 officers to the Confederate Army, and Virginia Military Institute provided 425. In the North, Norwich University furnished 523 officers to the Union Army, almost as many as West Point.

The lack of trained officers in the North was the main reason for the introduction of military instruction in the curricula of the colleges and universities under the terms of the Land Grant Act of 1862. This bill, sponsored by Justin Morrill of Vermont in the House of Representatives, provided for military instruction as part of the curriculum in those institutions. Instead of a large standing Regular Army, he proposed training in civilian educational institutions as a method by which a democratic people could gain a competent Officer Corps for the military reserve without endangering basic liberties.

The Land Grant Act offered to each state tracts of public lands. The funds derived from their sale were to be devoted to "the endowment, support and maintenance of at least one college where the leading subject shall be, without excluding other scientific and classical studies, and including military tactics, to teach such branches of learning as are related to agriculture and the mechanic arts ... " This measure not only helped the states establish colleges in new areas where people were settling, but it also broadened public support for advanced education.

The military program was conducted differently in each land-grant school. In the beginning, it was uncertain whether the Act called for military training as a compulsory or an optional course of study. Neither Congress nor the War Department clarified the matter. It was left to each college to determine the extent of military training that would be conducted. As a result, military instruction varied from no requirement to a four-year required course. Generally, the instruction consisted only of drill. Even when officers were assigned to colleges as Professors of Military Science, they were not furnished courses or study material but were required to develop programs with the college faculty.

Unfortunately, the Morrill Act contained no provision for assisting the land-grant institutions to conduct military instruction. As a consequence, such instruction became an additional course to be given by faculty members with previous military training. To rectify this situation, legislation was enacted in 1866, 1888, and 1891 authorizing the War Department to assign Regular Army officers as instructors at land-grant institutions and military colleges such as Norwich. The program grew slowly, however. In 1898 only 42 institutions had military departments with military instruction. The largest enrollment at any school was at the University of California.

Although the pre-ROTC system of military education on civilian campuses lacked provision for a formal officer reserve, it apparently accomplished a good deal more than has been generally recognized. Until 1898 most of the Army officers assigned to the colleges were mature West Point graduates, more than half of those so assigned in 1897 having had twenty years or more of active service. How many other students of the pre-1898 period served in the Army and Navy during and after the war with Spain has never been calculated. More than a hundred were commissioned in the Regular Army, and at least 1,345 officers on active Army duty as regulars or volunteers had trained in land-grant schools. The University of Nebraska battalion, about 360 strong, which as the 1st Nebraska Volunteer Infantry served with distinction in the Philippines, was but one of a number of land-grant cadet units that formed whole battalions or companies in the volunteer Army. Upon declaration of war in April 1898, the Army withdrew its officers detailed to the colleges, and years passed before the program regained the vitality that it had developed on the eve of the war with Spain.

Between the Spanish-American War and World War I, the military policy of the United States called for the establishment of an effective and rational system of military preparedness and the creation of a federally controlled reserve force. To supply young college-trained reserve officers to the new reserve force, the Reserve Officers Training Corps was created.

To develop this reserve force, considerable attention was focused on the military training conducted in land-grant colleges. A practice was adopted shortly after the Spanish-American War of granting "Distinguished Institution" ratings annually to the top ten land-grant and military colleges as determined by War Department inspection reports. One outstanding student was selected from each college and recommended for a commission in the Regular Army. By 1912, minimum training standards in land-grant and military colleges had been the subject of a conference in Washington between college officials and representatives of the War Department.

The foundation of the modern ROTC program was laid by the National Defense Act of 1916. This Act recognized colleges and universities, with the land-grant institutions as the nucleus, as the most promising source of future college-trained officers. At the same time, it provided for an extensive reserve system based on state National Guard units (the former state militia). The federal government assumed responsibility for equipping, training, and paying the National Guard units, but the units were required to meet federal standards of efficiency and were liable for federal service in the event of an emergency. This followed the United States military concept that federally recognized National Guard units were the first line of defense behind the Regular Army. In addition, the Act created an organized Reserve Corps for which officers would generally be trained in a War Department–approved ROTC organization. Graduates of the ROTC were appointed Second Lieutenants, organized Reserve Corps.

Instead of the four years of military education and training that had customarily been required of all physically qualified male students in land-grant institutions, the ROTC plan called for two years of basic training, compulsory at the option of the institution, and two years of advanced training for selected students only. The government would furnish uniforms as well as instruction and equipment for all students in training, while the schools themselves would continue to be responsible for providing the classrooms, drill halls, and other facilities needed for training purposes. The new advanced course included six weeks of summer camp instruction, and advanced students were to be compensated and assured of reserve commissions on satisfactory completion of the course.

The declaration of war in April 1917 prevented a fair test of the ROTC system until the 1920's, but prewar military training in colleges and universities more than proved its worth. The land-grant institutions alone contributed more than 100,000 graduates and former students to the armed forces in World War I, of whom at least 30,000 became officers. It is believed that a large proportion of the nearly 90,000 members of the Officers Reserve Corps transferred to active duty during the war had received military instruction in civilian institutions of higher learning. What mattered most was the existence at the outset of a large nucleus of trained civilian reserve officers, without which the United States Army could never have grown so rapidly in 1917, or played the decisive role in France in 1918 that it actually did.

With the end of World War I, the War Department took steps to reconstitute and expand the ROTC program at civilian educational institutions. By June 1919, Army ROTC units had been established in 191 colleges and universities, almost twice the number that had been operating when we entered the war. In 1920, Air Corps (then Air Service) ROTC units were established at the University of California, the University of Illinois, the Massachusetts Institute of Technology, and Texas A & M. This expansion broadened the association of military personnel with higher education. Army officers were assigned to ROTC duty in increasing numbers. The majority of cadets were still in land-grant and military colleges, although units were also being operated in privately endowed colleges and universities. The program was organized in two parts, basic and advanced, each normally covering two years of college. Enrollment in basic ROTC was compulsory in the land-grant colleges and some private institutions. Advanced ROTC was on a selective and completely voluntary basis and led to a reserve commission for those successfully completing the course.

After an initial period of great activity, the ROTC program began to decline as the nation turned its attention away from problems of national security. Some universities considered dropping the compulsory features. Pacifist agitation in the 1930's became quite extensive, and there was considerable discussion of the role of ROTC. However, the opposition to ROTC at this time in no way compared to what would occur some forty years later when ROTC on campus became the focal point of opposition to the Vietnam War. At this time, however, most educational institutions continued to favor compulsory ROTC. By the mid-1930's, only seventeen colleges had dropped ROTC altogether and seven had changed from compulsory to elective programs. For budgetary reasons because of the Depression, separate Air ROTC Units were discontinued in 1935.

During this period, the main duty of ROTC graduates was to staff the organized Reserve Corps. At the same time, opportunities for Reserve officers to go on active-duty training increased with the passage of the Thomason Act in 1935. This act provided that up to 1,000 Reserve officers could train with the Regular Army for one year and that 50 could be offered Regular Army commissions at the end of the training period. Another opportunity for active duty for the ROTC-graduated Reserve officer occurred when the Army took over the organization and administration of the Civilian Conservation Corps camps.

The small Navy ROTC program, which had been established in six institutions in 1926, began to expand in the late 1930's. By the time the United States moved into its prewar mobilization stage, the number of Navy ROTC units had increased to 27. As a result, when the United States began its rearming program, over 100,000 Reserve officers were available for active duty with the Army and more than 2,000 with the Navy, most of whom were ROTC graduates. The Army Chief of Staff, General George C. Marshall, commenting on the contribution of ROTC in World War II, said, "The most valuable asset we have had in this emergency has been the product of the ROTC. Just what we would have done in the early phases of our mobilization and training without these men I do not know. I do know that our plans would have had to be greatly curtailed and the cessation of hostilities on the European Front would have been delayed accordingly." ROTC contributed significantly to US success in World War II just as it had in World War I.

When the Selective Service Act was passed in 1940, ROTC students were exempt from registering for military service, but as in World War I, World War II suspended the ROTC program. The Army ROTC program was maintained until 1943, but thereafter the Army relied on graduates of the Officer Candidate Schools to meet the officer shortage, since these schools could train officers faster in a short, intensified course. In June 1943, the Navy established the V-12 program (an Officer Candidate program) by absorbing students in the Navy ROTC and two smaller reserve programs, the V-1

and V-7. This program was designed to meet the Navy's officer requirements, but it also provided continuity from the wartime program to the reestablishment of Navy ROTC units.

At the end of World War II, the majority of the Army officers at company and battalion level were former ROTC cadets. In the five combat divisions that were polled, the following percentages were Reserve Officers: 52 percent of the Lieutenant Colonels, 82.5 percent of the Majors, 70 percent of the Captains, 26.8 percent of the First Lieutenants, and 9.3 percent of the Second Lieutenants. Of these Reserve officers, 90 percent were ROTC graduates.

During the period 1945 to 1950, the Reserve Officers Training Corps programs underwent many important changes. It was during the early postwar years that the National Security Act of 1947 became law. Under Title II, the United States Air Force was established and placed on equal status with the Army and Navy. The Air Force promptly undertook to develop an ROTC program that would be responsive to its own requirements.

The Air Force needed officers who were technically qualified to operate increasingly complicated equipment and were also trained to understand the field of air capabilities. In addition to training air crews, it had to develop a curriculum to produce graduates who were qualified in nonflying activities, such as communications and aircraft maintenance, essential to Air Force needs. Except for Academy graduates, Air Force officer positions were largely filled by Regular and Reserve officers who had entered the service through the Aviation Cadet program. Since many were without college degrees, the Air Force initiated a program to raise the educational level of these officers. The postwar ROTC program became a central element in recruiting Air Force officers. In 1946, while still a part of the Army, the Air Force had established its own ROTC units on 78 college and university campuses. From a total enrollment of 8,756 officer candidates in 1946–47, the number increased to 40,658 in 1948–49 and over 47,000 in 127 institutions in 1949–50.

Meanwhile, the Army and Navy had been developing postwar ROTC plans. Early in 1945, Congress authorized the Navy to enroll 24,000 students in Navy ROTC during the period of wartime emergency and to increase the number of ROTC students from the peacetime authorization of 7,200 to a postwar level of 14,000. The Navy contacted colleges and universities shortly after the passage of this legislation to discuss the expanded program. Initially, it was planned to convert V-12 units into Navy ROTC units without inter-

ruption. When the war ended, the Navy was conducting ROTC/V-12 training at 66 colleges and universities.

In October 1945, the Secretary of the Navy approved a report prepared by a board of naval officers headed by Rear Admiral Holloway. That report laid the foundation for the Navy's postwar ROTC program. The main recommendations provided for subsidized education of Navy ROTC midshipmen for the Regular Navy and Marine Corps, who were to be selected by competitive examination. As approved by the Congress in July 1946, and signed by the President, the bill authorized a total enrollment of 15,400 midshipmen in the Navy ROTC program, with not more than 14,000 midshipmen whose education could be subsidized. Although the number of subsidized students never exceeded 7,000 at the time because of budgetary limitations, the difference between 15,400 and the number of subsidized students would be known as "contract" students. By 1950, the Holloway Plan was operating on 52 campuses and the Navy had approximately 6,800 subsidized students and 3,900 contract students enrolled.

The Army was also prepared to resume ROTC training in colleges and universities during the early postwar years. Initially, it reactivated the Advanced ROTC course in those institutions that had had Army ROTC prior to World War II, although the enrollment was limited to 10,000 students. The Army received congressional authorization to credit students having adequate prior military service with the basic two-year course. By the time colleges and universities opened in the fall of 1945, the Army ROTC program had been established on 129 campuses. By the spring of 1950, the Army's four-year ROTC program was in full operation on 190 campuses with an enrollment of over 100,000 students. In one direction ROTC training in land-grant institutions was extended into an area where it had never existed before. ROTC had not included the separate Negro land-grant schools established in the South. The Army broke the spell in 1948 by organizing units at three Negro institutions, and currently it maintains units at 21 historically black institutions. The Army also, along with the other services, commissions many black ROTC graduates from other colleges and universities across the nation.

The sudden attack on the Republic of Korea in 1950 caused disruption in the ROTC training programs of all the services, but not as significant a disruption as had occurred in 1898, 1917, and 1941. The Army, Navy, and Air Force all made conscious decisions to expand their ROTC programs to fill the increasing requirements for active-duty officers. The Korean War period marked the transformation of the ROTC program from a reserve to an active-duty training program for all three services. This change in direction has been the mark of the program up to the present day.

The passage of the Universal Military Training and Service Act of 1951 assisted all three services in expanding their programs. For the first time we were to have compulsory military training in peacetime. The Act provided that every able-bodied young man would be liable for military service for eight years, two of which would be served on active duty. In the beginning, ROTC students received special deferment privileges, but owing to the heavy requirements for active-duty personnel in the initial phases of the conflict, the deferment policy was altered. Army and Air Force ROTC cadets and Navy contract students, after completing their sophomore year, had to agree to serve on extended active duty for at least two years after graduating and being commissioned. Those who would not sign the agreement were immediately dropped from the ROTC programs and were liable for the draft as enlisted personnel.

ROTC performed a great service to the nation during the Korean conflict by providing large numbers of junior officers in all services who were quickly deployed overseas. Fortunately, the Korean conflict did not escalate into World War III, and an armistice was signed in July 1953. In the Army program, great numbers of ROTC graduates were commissioned in 1955 and 1956 as a result of the expansion of the program. However, as a result of the termination of hostilities, no active-duty positions were available for many of the newly commissioned graduates. It was finally determined in 1955 that Army ROTC graduates who could not be assigned to a two-year active-duty tour could be placed on active duty for a six-month training period and released with an obligation to serve on reserve duty for seven and a half years. Army officer production through the ROTC program showed a slight decrease from a high of 15,173 in 1954 to a low of 10,014 in 1966. At that time, the figures started to show an increase as a result of the impact of the Vietnam War, and the initial support of that conflict in 1963–65 was reflected in increased numbers until 1972. In many ways the ROTC programs of all services became symbols of the United States' involvement in an increasingly unpopular war in Southeast Asia, and this factor along with other social factors in the late 1960's and early 1970's caused a sharp decrease in ROTC enrollments.The Army ROTC program produced only 4,606 officers in 1976—the lowest figure since the years immediately after World War II. Fortunately for the nation, the image of military officers and the military in general has improved dramatically since the early 70's and our involvement in Vietnam. Production figures for all services are on the increase.

The Air Force ROTC program was already expanding in the early 1950's, and the outbreak of hostilities in Korea and the almost immediate commitment of US forces further expanded the program and increased the emphasis on training active-duty and career officers. The expansion of the Air Force in the early 1950's required the Air Force ROTC program to produce more and more officers who would be trained to become flying personnel. Changes were also introduced in the obligated tour of military service for ROTC graduates. For the first time, in 1951, students completing their sophomore year had to agree to serve on extended duty for two years before being commissioned in the reserves. The Air Force ROTC program was confronted with new policy and strategic requirements. It soon became apparent that technological innovations had brought new weapons and techniques that could not be fully exploited by short-term officers. The conversion of the ROTC program from training officers for the reserve to recruiting active-duty officers did not fulfill the new requirements. If most of the young AFROTC officers chose to return to civil life on completion of their obligated tours of active duty, the Air Force could not meet its professional needs. In 1954, the Air Force drastically reduced the number of students in nonflying categories. In 1957, the Air Force required graduates in both pilot and navigator categories to serve on active duty for five years after being commissioned. The Air Force also underwent experiences similar to the Army in the production of graduates during the turbulent times of the late 1960's and the early 1970's. There was an increase in Air Force ROTC enrollments during the first years of the US involvement in Vietnam, but enrollments dropped off starting in 1969 and continued to decrease until 1976. Then the pendulum swung back the other way, and like the other services, Air Force enrollments are once again on the increase.

In 1956 the Air Force experimented with a program to allow women in the Air Force ROTC program at selected colleges. The program was discontinued in 1960. Women were again enrolled on a full-time basis in 1969. Women were awarded scholarships in ROTC beginning in 1970.

The Navy ROTC program was the one least affected by the Korean conflict. The Navy had planned to expand the output of Officer Candidate Schools if there were a requirement for active-duty officers over and above those coming from regular sources. All services were confronted with the need for more active-duty officers. It will be recalled that all ROTC students, under the 1951 Act, were initially placed in a deferred status until completion of their sophomore year. This Act included students in the Navy ROTC contract program. Students in this category were obligated to serve on extended active duty for two years after being commissioned in the Reserves, or they were dropped from the program and became subject to the draft.

By 1950, the first full classes of regular NROTC graduates were being commissioned. These students had been enrolled under the congressional authorization passed in 1946, which established NROTC as a source of officers for the Regular Navy. The graduates were obligated to go on active duty immediately after receiving their baccalaureate degree. As a result of the war in Korea, the "regular" NROTC graduates were required to serve three years in the Reserves after being commissioned. After the war, many ROTC-trained officers left the service when they had completed their obligated tour of duty. For example, the class of 1950, which was the first full-strength class to graduate under the Holloway Plan, produced almost 1,000 Ensigns, but by 1960 only 100 were still on active duty. Of the 1,118 NROTC graduates in 1954, only 195 were still on duty in 1963.

This rapid turnover in personnel, which became apparent to the Navy in the mid-1950's, created many significant personnel manning and experience problems. It was therefore decided that all regular students entering NROTC training, beginning with the fall term of 1957, would be required to serve four years on active duty. In addition, all NROTC regular and contract students who went into the Flight Training Program were obligated to serve three and a half years on active duty after completion of the flight training course of eighteen months.

The Navy also experienced periods of turbulence in its ROTC program in the late 1960's and early 1970's. There were scattered demonstrations and protests against ROTC on academic campuses. ROTC was a visible symbol of US participation in the Vietnam War, and the program came under attack by some elements of the population. Enrollments in the Navy ROTC program decreased in this period of social unrest, but as in the other services, enrollments started to increase in the late 1970's.

The period from 1963 to 1973, which roughly coincides with US support and military involvement in Vietnam, was a period of great change in the structure of the ROTC programs as well as in the public perception of the programs. It became increasingly clear that

ROTC was to reverse its role permanently so that it would become the main source of active-duty officers in all the services. The awareness of the growing importance of ROTC to the security of the nation prompted congressional action to authorize additional appropriations for the ROTC program, to attract not only more people but also highly qualified people.

In 1964, Congress passed the ROTC Vitalization Act, which authorized scholarships for all service ROTC programs, the expansion of all junior ROTC programs, and the start of two-year programs along with the four-year program. In 1965 and again in 1971 the subsistence allowance was increased. The allowance today for all ROTC programs is $100 a month tax-free for scholarship students and students in the last two years of the program. The expansion of the program took the form of new agreements with colleges and universities to offer ROTC instruction on campuses away from the ROTC host institutions in crosstown and cross-enrolled agreements. Expansion occurred by actively encouraging more women to join the ROTC program in all the services. The importance of the junior ROTC program was recognized, and efforts were made to increase enrollment by publicizing the program, and also by appealing more to women high school students. These changes were initially well received by the public, but as we have seen, support of US involvement in the war in Southeast Asia began to decrease noticeably in the late 1960's and early 1970's. As a consequence, public support and acceptance of the ROTC programs also decreased. Enrollment dropped in the early 1970's, and ROTC became a focal point of student demonstrations against the war in Vietnam on some college campuses. After the end of US involvement in Vietnam, the government began the difficult process of restoring the public's faith in the ROTC program and actively seeking its support in increasing the enrollment of young people in the program.

The year 1973 marks the start of the modern service ROTC programs. In that year the draft was abolished. Male US citizens are still required to register upon reaching their eighteenth birthday, but men are no longer subject to be drafted to serve two years of active duty. There has been much discussion of reinstituting the draft to fulfill manpower requirements in the armed forces, but opposition is considerable. It is unlikely that the United States will return to conscription unless it is required by a national emergency.

The end of the draft caused a marked change in all the service ROTC programs. All programs must now compete more openly for eligible men and women. All services must attempt to make military careers more attractive to potential applicants. This competition affects not only the ROTC programs but the enlisted recruiting programs as well. Demographics indicate that the available personnel pool will decrease in the next ten years. Therefore, the military will have to compete with industry, business, academia, agriculture, service industries, and many other sectors of the economy for manpower resources. The bottom line is that ROTC offers more benefits, scholarships, and special programs today than at any time in its history.

All services have increased the number of scholarships available to both high school and college students. Many new scholarships have been created to attract people with specialized skills such as medical, dental,veterinary, nursing, and law specialties. Efforts have been made to attract active-duty enlisted personnel to the ROTC program so that they will complete their college education, complete ROTC requirements, be commissioned, and serve as officers.

Opportunities are much greater for ROTC graduates to be granted a regular commission if they are so inclined. Active duty is almost guaranteed for Air Force and Navy ROTC graduates, and it is available to Army ROTC graduates who distinguish themselves in the program. In an effort to increase enrollments, the Army initiated a Guaranteed Reserve Forces Program in 1979. A nonscholarship Army ROTC cadet can request reserve status after completing the program. All services are attempting to place ROTC participants in desired positions, provided the needs of the service can be met.

All the service programs have become more concerned with the quality of the overall education received. Many ROTC detachments actively assist students by providing tutoring and support with the academic curriculum. All services have become more sensitive to the competing demands placed on students by academic and ROTC requirements, and more mutually beneficial accommodations have been worked out.

For the foreseeable future, the United States will require a military force for its security. Whom do we want to lead our Armed Forces? Both common sense and history tell us that the larger interests of a free society are best served by military officers who stem from the society they serve, share its values, are broadly representative of the best that is in us, reflect the richness of our diverse origins, and are committed to the great and common purposes of our nation.

Today, the vast majority of the people commissioned in the service ROTC programs do not make the military a lifetime career.

They serve on active duty for a short period and then return to civilian life. They bring new ideas, new perspectives, and a productive vitality to our armed forces. They return to civilian life, perhaps to continue to serve in the reserve forces, having gained hands-on leadership experience, managerial skills, a sense of responsibility and service, and tremendous self-confidence from the military experience. This pool of reserve leadership will serve our country well in the event of a national emergency—who better is there to defend the country?

Chapter **IV**

The Army ROTC Program

Overview

Army ROTC is the primary source for college-trained officers for the US Army, the Army Reserve, and the Army National Guard. Army ROTC is currently offered at over 300 host institutions, over 100 extension centers, and over 1,000 colleges and universities under cross-enrollment agreements. These ROTC colleges and universities are located in all fifty states, the District of Columbia, Puerto Rico, and Guam.

Army ROTC is a four-year program divided into two parts, the basic course and the advanced course. The basic course is normally attended during the freshman and sophomore years. No military commitment is incurred in the basic course for nonscholarship cadets; the student may withdraw at any time before the beginning of the third year. Subjects taught include Communications, Land Navigation, Military History, Leadership Development, Drill and Ceremonies, Military Courtesy, Discipline, and Customs. Uniforms, necessary textbooks, and materials are furnished without cost.

After completing this course, selected students may enroll in the advanced course during the final two years of college. Instruction in this program includes further Leadership Development, Small Unit Tactics, Ethics and Professionalism, Principles of War, and Military Justice. Cadets in the advanced course receive uniforms, necessary Military Science textbooks, salary during an advanced camp, and a subsistence allowance of up to $1,000 each year.

Cadets are scheduled for a six-week advanced camp held during the summer between the junior and senior years. This camp permits cadets to put into practice the principles and theories they have acquired in the classroom. Successful completion of the advanced camp is required prior to receiving a commission.

A special two-year program is available for community and junior college graduates and students at four-year colleges who have not taken part in Army ROTC during their first two years. Students can enter this program by successfully completing a six-week basic camp, for which they receive pay, to qualify for enrollment in the advanced course. Obligations incurred and requirements for the two- and four-year programs are the same except for basic camp attendance.

Army ROTC offers scholarships for five, four, three, and two years. Applications for the nationwide scholarships are available after April 1 each year from Army ROTC, PO Box 9000, Clifton, NJ 07015-9974.

Five-year and four-year scholarships are awarded on a nationwide competitive basis to US citizens who will be entering college as freshmen. Both men and women are eligible to compete. Three-year and two-year scholarships are awarded competitively to students who are already enrolled in college. Students who attend basic camp before entering the two-year program may also compete for two-year scholarships while at camp. Three- and two-year scholarships are available for active-duty Army enlisted personnel on a competitive basis. All ROTC scholarships pay tuition; provide flat-rate fees for textbooks, supplies and equipment, on-campus lab fees, and other purely educational expenses, and provide a subsistence allow-

Classroom navigation work at the ROTC unit.

ance of up to $1,000 each year the scholarship is in effect. The value of the scholarship depends on the tuition and other educational costs of the school attended. There is no monetary limit on the amount of tuition the Army will pay for scholarships. Consequently, the Army will pick up full tuition for students who are awarded scholarships and have been accepted to an institution that offers a four-year Army ROTC program.

Five-year and four-year scholarship recipients incur a military obligation at the beginning of their sophomore year. Three- and two-year scholarship recipients incur a military obligation concurrently with the commencement of their scholarship benefits.

Under the ROTC Reserve Forces Duty Scholarship Program, a limited number of two-year scholarships are also available to students who wish to serve with the Army Reserves in lieu of extended active duty. Special provisions allow for selected nursing students to qualify for appointment in the Army Nurse Corps through ROTC.

Under the Simultaneous Membership Program (SMP), a non-scholarship college student can combine service in the Army Reserves or National Guard as an officer trainee with participation in ROTC and be paid for both. Details about the Army ROTC program may be obtained at the Army ROTC detachment at participating universities or by writing to Army ROTC, Fort Monroe, VA 23651.

Mission

The Army, along with the Air Force, Navy, and Marine Corps, has one fundamental mission: to provide for the security of the United States and for the support of US national and international policies. The ultimate purpose of all military training is to prepare personnel to carry out efficiently and expeditiously their service responsibilities. Title 10, United States Code, Section 3062, states in part:

> "It is the intent of Congress to provide an Army that is capable, in conjunction with the other armed forces, of preserving the peace and security ... of the United States; .. supporting the national policies; .. implementing the national objectives; .. and overcoming any nations responsible for aggressive acts that imperil the peace and security of the United States."

The fundamental role of the Army, as the Nation's land force, is to defeat enemy forces in land combat and to gain control of the land and its people.

As has been discussed previously, it is the traditional policy of the

United States to maintain active armed forces of a size consistent with the immediate security needs of the nation. In the event of an emergency, the armed forces must have the capability of rapid expansion, and therefore military leaders and specialists must be trained during peacetime. The greatest percentage of these trained leaders is provided by the ROTC program.

The role of Army ROTC is to continue to be the primary source of junior officers for the total Army—the Regular Army, the Army National Guard, and the US Army Reserve. This mission will grow as the total Army moves ahead with its modernization programs and increases its need for highly motivated, technically skilled junior officers. Army ROTC insures a continuing flow of qualified personnel into the Officer Corps of the Army, conducts precommissioning and basic military training programs, stimulates interest in military careers, promotes appreciation of the Army as a service, encourages paticipation in the Reserve components of the Army, assists educational institutions in the development of maturity in students, and represents the Army at the academic institutions and the surrounding community.

Organization and Administration

The main focus of the Army ROTC program is the senior division program, whose purpose is to procure and train college students so that they may qualify upon graduation as commissioned officers in the Army of the United States. Army ROTC also has a junior division ROTC program that is conducted at the high school level. The purpose of the junior program is to provide military training at the high school level that will benefit the student and the Army; no obligations are incurred by participation. The Junior ROTC program is discussed separately later in this chapter.

Like any military organization, Army ROTC works through a chain of command, with overall direction given by the Deputy Chief of Staff for ROTC, who is on the staff of the Commanding General, US Army Training and Doctrine Command, Fort Monroe, Virginia. The Deputy Chief of Staff for ROTC also serves as the Commander of the Reserve Officers Training Corps. In this capacity, he commands four Region Commanders, who, in turn, are charged with the success of the program in their geographic area. The First ROTC Region is headquartered at Fort Bragg, North Carolina, and includes Maine, New Hampshire, Vermont, Massachusetts, Rhode Island, Connecticut, New York, Pennsylvania, New Jersey, Delaware, Maryland, Virginia, North and South Carolina, Georgia, Florida, the District of Columbia, Puerto Rico, Virgin Islands, and

Panama. The Second ROTC Region is headquartered at Fort Knox, Kentucky, and includes Wisconsin, Michigan, Illinois, Indiana, Ohio, West Virginia, Kentucky, Tennessee, and Missouri. The Third ROTC Region is headquartered at Fort Riley, Kansas, and includes Kansas, Oklahoma, Arkansas, Mississippi, Alabama, Louisiana, Texas, and New Mexico. The Fourth ROTC Region is headquartered at Fort Lewis, Washington, and includes Washington, Idaho, North and South Dakota, Minnesota, Iowa, Nebraska, Colorado, Arizona, California, Nevada, Utah, Wyoming, Montana, Oregon, Alaska, Hawaii, American Samoa, and Guam.

The four Region Commanders, all Brigadier Generals, are assisted by Area Commanders, who have responsibility for supervising the Professor of Military Science at colleges and universities in their respective areas. A representative Senior ROTC detachment would include the Professor of Military Science, usually a Lieutenant Colonel; four assistant Professors of Military Science, usually three Captains and a Major; two drill instructors, usually a Sergeant Major and Master Sergeant; a Supply Sergeant, and an Administrative Sergeant. Most detachments have one or two civilian clerk-typists. The key player in the ROTC program is the Professor of Military Science (PMS), who is charged with recruiting students for the program, teaching the classes, retaining interest on the part of the cadets, and handling the variety of administrative functions associated with an on-campus program.

Most civilian heads of educational institutions having ROTC units generally exercise the same control over the Department of Military Science as they do over other departments of the school. The Military Science Department may be grouped with other service programs under a Military Studies Department, or it may be attached to one of the colleges in the university system. The Professor of Military Science is responsible both to school officials and to higher military authorities for the effective conduct and administration of all ROTC activities at his school. He also represents the Department of the Army locally in all matters relating to the ROTC. He and his staff are carefully selected to meet the high standards required of all personnel assigned to ROTC duty. The academic institutions usually furnish classroom facilities, administrative support, and academic accreditation for the ROTC program. Obviously, the better the relationship between the academic officials and the representatives of the ROTC program, the better chance that the program will be successful on campus.

Efforts are currently under way to upgrade the importance of ROTC in the Army and recognize the valuable contribution ROTC makes to the Nation. Increased Command emphasis and funding may result. This initiative is a logical step to mark the importance of the program and improve the overall operations.

The Junior ROTC Program

The Junior Reserve Officers Training Corps (JROTC) is designed to prepare high school students for responsible leadership roles and to make them aware of the opportunities and benefits of citizenship. JROTC began with the National Defense Act of 1916 with a mandate to teach high school students the principles of leadership and organizational know-how. In 1964 Congress passed the ROTC Vitalization Act, which permitted the Army to increase the JROTC units to a combined 1,200 units. The total was raised to 1,600 in 1966. The program has been expanded significantly in recent years. Today there are over 870 JROTC units nationwide with a total enrollment of approximately 135,000 cadets. The current expansion program gives priority to establishment of new units in states that have a low density of JROTC units.

JROTC is a cooperative program between a high school and the Army. There are units in forty-four states, Puerto Rico, American Samoa, Guam, and the US Virgin Islands. There are also JROTC units in the American communities in the Federal Republic of Germany, the Republic of Korea, and Panama. Programs are set up for three or four years with academic or technical subjects or both. The program teaches young men and women good citizenship, patriotism, self-reliance, leadership, respect for constituted authority, the ability to communicate effectively, the importance of physical fitness, the role of the Army in support of national interests and objectives, and basic military skills.

JROTC cadets are taught predominantly by retired Army officers and noncommissioned officers. The instruction takes students into areas they normally would not study in high school, and it often inspires them to excel in their academic classes. The end result is students who can think on their own, are sure of themselves, and express their ideas and opinions clearly and concisely. JROTC cadets learn to lead and motivate others. Many enter the senior ROTC program in college, attend one of the military academies, or enter the service in an enlisted status.

In addition to the JROTC units, two National Defense Cadet Corps (NDCC) detachments are active in Pennsylvania. The NDCC began in 1916 as a result of the National Defense Act and shares the philosophy and objectives of JROTC. The NDCC differs in that less Army support is offered the program.

Scholarships

To attract the best-qualified students, the Army offers a wide variety of scholarships to ROTC cadets. Merit scholarships are awarded in sixteen categories and are available to graduating high school students, those already in college, and to members of the total Army serving either on active duty or with a reserve component. All scholarships are awarded on a competitive basis. Four-year scholarships are awarded to students who will be entering college as freshmen. Three- and two-year scholarships are awarded to students already enrolled in college and to Army enlisted personnel on active duty. Students who attend the basic camp of the two-year program may compete for two-year scholarships while at camp.

The Army has a continuing need to commission officers with backgrounds in the sciences, engineering, nursing, and other technical areas. The following guidelines are in effect for awarding scholarships for the immediate future: Engineering, 30 percent; Social Studies, 10 percent; Physical Science, 25 percent; Nursing, 7 percent; Business, 20 percent; and other disciplines, 8 percent.

The most widely known and sought-after scholarships are the four-year awards, which are reserved for high school graduates who will be enrolling in college for the first time. Competition is keen, with approximately nine applications received for every scholarship available. At present, approximately 1,500 new four-year scholarships are available each year. From 1980 to 1985 the number of applications for all scholarships increased by more than 62 percent, from 10,750 in school year 1980–81 to 17,350 in 1984–85. The number of total scholarships has grown from 6,500 in 1980–81 to the 12,000 ceiling currently in effect. The 12,000 ceiling should allow the awarding of between 4,000 and 4,700 new scholarships each year. The value of the ROTC scholarship to the individual varies depending on the tuition cost at the school attended and the length of the award. If the student attends an Army-approved school, there is no upper limit to the amount of tuition the Army will fund.

An innovation for school year 1985–86 was that many four-year scholarship alternates not offered scholarships during their first academic term of a given school year were given an opportunity for a scholarship without reapplying. Alternates now have a three-year award reserved for them providing that they still meet medical standards, basic eligibility requirements, and specific academic and ROTC performance requirements. The student must have taken the first year of the ROTC program and performed well.

Also planned for 1985–86 was a possible one-year extension of the scholarship if the academic discipline required more than four years to earn an undergraduate degree. Each such application would be reviewed individually, could be made only after a minimum of one-year college performance, and would be contingent upon successful progress toward the degree. Four-year scholarship cadets receiving additional benefits would incur a longer active-duty obligation. Three- and two-year cadets would also have an opportunity to apply for extended benefits.

The government has a large investment in each cadet who attends college on an ROTC scholarship. To ensure maximum retention of scholarship cadets, the military obligation commitment begins at the start of the sophomore year. Under this policy, only first-year cadets are permitted to withdraw from ROTC. Those who withdraw later may be obligated to repay the cost of benefits received or to serve on active duty in an enlisted status. These restrictions apply only to scholarship cadets; nonscholarship cadets are under no obligation to the Army until they sign a contract entering their junior year.

Other features of the ROTC scholarship system are the Quality Enrichment Program (QEP) for high school graduates who attend one of the Historically Black Colleges hosting ROTC, scholarships to attend military and military junior colleges (listed in the Appendix), and scholarships earned for outstanding performance in basic camp. Each of the six military junior colleges that host Army ROTC has up to ten scholarships available annually for high school graduates. Basic camp scholarships are for two years and are awarded to persons who excel at the summer program at Fort Knox, Kentucky. Four hundred scholarships were awarded for 1984–85, with a number reserved for cadets who agree to serve with the Reserve components upon commissioning. Although not a separate program, a number of scholarships are specifically designed for qualified nursing students.

PROFILE OF SY 84-85 ARMY ROTC 4-YEAR
NATIONAL SCHOLARSHIP WINNERS

PERCENTAGE

Top 15 Percent of Class	87
Number 1 or 2 in Class	19
Varsity Team Captains	28
National Honor Society Members	67
Club Presidents	33
Varsity Letter Winners	72
State Organization Participants	41
Presidents of Student Body or Senior Class or other Class Officials	77

COLLEGE BOARD SCORES

1400-1600	14 percent
1000-1399	83 percent
850-999	3 percent

MEAN SCORE - 1240
(High School National Mean 894)
MEAN CLASS STANDING - 20 of 290

ROTC SCHOLARSHIPS BY TYPES AND LENGTHS

Four-Year National
    Early Cycle and Regular Cycle awarded to highly qualified high
    school graduates in national competition.

Four-Year Quality Enrichment
    Awarded only to those qualified high school graduates planning
    to attend one of the Historically Black Colleges hosting Army
    ROTC.

*Three-Year National Enrolled
    Applicants presently enrolled in ROTC.

*Three-Year National Nonenrolled
    Applicants not presently enrolled in ROTC but attending college.

Three-Year Active Duty
Applicants are active duty Army soldiers with one year of college credits. Awarded in Army-wide competition.

*Three-Year Allocation
Allocated to ROTC Regions to provide nominees in specific desired academic disciplines.

Three-Year Minority Incentive
For institutions having the largest increase in MS III minority students over the previous year.

*Two-Year National Enrolled
Applicants presently enrolled in ROTC.

*Two-Year National Nonenrolled
Applicants not presently enrolled in ROTC, but attending college.

*Two-Year Allocation
Allocated to ROTC Regions to provide nominees in specific desired academic disciplines.

Two-Year Basic Camp
Awarded to those applying at Basic Camp and based on camp performance and leadership qualifications.

Two-Year Active Duty
Awarded to active Army soldiers who have completed two years of college.

Two-Year Reserve Forces Duty
Awarded to members or potential members of the Army National Guard and US Army Reserve.

Two-Year Military College (MC)
Awarded to students attending Military Colleges.

Two-Year Military Junior College (MJC)
Awarded to high school graduates who signify their intention to enroll in an MJC.

Scholarships include payment of tuition, a flat rate for books, supplies, equipment, and certain other educational expenses, plus

---

*On-campus program.

up to $1,000 subsistence allowance per academic year, paid at the rate of $100 per month for each year the scholarship is in effect and ROTC instruction is being received. All scholarship students will be required to serve in the military for a period of 8 years. This obligation may be fulfilled by serving 2 to 4 years on active duty followed by service in the Army National Guard or United States Army Reserve, or by serving 8 years in the Army National Guard or United States Army Reserve preceded by a 3- to 6-month active duty period. Four-year scholarship cadets receiving extended scholarship benefits (5 years of scholarship assistance) will incur a 5-year active duty obligation as opposed to 2 to 4 years.

Qualifications and Requirements

To qualify for a four-year Army ROTC scholarship you must:

- Be a citizen of the United States when you accept the award.
- Be at least seventeen years old before the scholarship becomes effective.
- Take either the Scholastic Aptitude Test (SAT) or the American College Test (ACT) no later than December of the year you apply for the scholarship. Army ROTC must be listed as a test score recipient by the use of Code 0454 for the SAT and Code 1676 for the ACT.
- Have good high school grades.
- Participate in leadership, extracurricular, and athletic activities. Students who hold part-time jobs and do not have time to participate in these activities will be given substitute credit based upon the number of hours worked per week.
- Meet required physical standards.
- Be under twenty-five years old on June 30 of the year you expect to graduate and receive your officer's commission. (An age extension of up to four years may be possible for veterans who qualify.)
- Be a high school graduate or have equivalent credit.
- Be accepted by one of the colleges or universities that host a four-year Army ROTC program. (Four-year scholarships cannot be used at cross-enrolled schools or extension centers.)
- Pursue a Department of the Army–approved academic discipline.
- Successfully complete at least one quarter/semester of college instruction in a major Indo-European or Asian language.

- Agree to accept a commission as either a Regular Army, Army National Guard, or US Army Reserve officer, whichever is offered.

Once you have accepted a four-year Army ROTC scholarship and it becomes effective, you will be required to complete all the requirements to obtain your college degree and your officer's commission.

During and at the close of the application period, the best-qualified applicants are required to travel to a nearby Army installation or ROTC host college or university, at their own expense, for a personal interview and Physical Aptitude Examination (PAE) by Army representatives. Results of the interview and examination are forwarded to the United States Army Training and Doctrine Command at Fort Monroe, Virginia, where final selections are made. The selection of winners is based on:

- The results of the SAT and ACT tests.
- High school academic standing.
- Extracurricular, leadership, and athletic activities.
- A personal interview by a board of Army officers and a Physical Aptitude Examination. (The interview and PAE do not ensure that applicants will be selected for final scholarship consideration.)

How to Apply

The period for requesting application forms for four-year Army ROTC scholarships is from April 1 through November 15. If your completed application is received by August 15, you will be considered by a selection board for an early scholarship. Winners are announced about November 1. If your application is received after August 15 or if you were not selected by the first board, you will be considered in a later cycle. Applications for the later cycle must be received by the first working day in December and are reviewed by a different selection board. Winners are announced the following March. To obtain application forms and additional information, write to: Army ROTC, PO Box 9000, Clifton, NJ 07015-9974.

You may apply for a Quality Enrichment Program (QEP) four-year scholarship if you wish to attend a Historically Black College (HBC) that hosts the Army ROTC program. A limited number of these scholarships are awarded each year. To qualify, you must meet the same eligibility requirements as for the four-year scholarship. If you are awarded a QEP scholarship, you will be required to attend one of the twenty-one Historically Black Colleges. The same application forms are used as for a four-year scholarship. Applications should be requested between April 1 and November 15 from Army ROTC, PO Box 9000, Clifton, NJ 07015-9974.

If you have already completed one or two years of college, you may be eligible for a three- or two-year Army ROTC scholarship. Active-duty Army enlisted personnel who have completed one or two years of college may also be eligible. If you are a student attending basic camp as part of the two-year program, you may compete for a two-year scholarship while at camp. Three- and two-year scholarships may be used at any college or university where ROTC instruction is available. To qualify as an applicant for a three- or two-year scholarship, you must:

- Meet the same citizenship, age, and physical requirements as for a four-year scholarship.
- Have at least three years (for a three-year scholarship) or two years (for a two-year scholarship) remaining for your baccalaureate degree.
- Have satisfactory grades in all academic courses and ROTC courses (if already enrolled in ROTC).
- Be recommended by the Professor of Military Science (with the exception of basic camp applicants).

Three- and two-year Army ROTC scholarships are awarded on the following criteria:

- Your performance in your academic studies and, if you are enrolled in ROTC, your Military Science studies.
- Successfully passing the Physical Aptitude Examination or Army Physical Readiness Test. (All candidates are informed of the requirements of each physical examination prior to taking the exam.)
- A personal interview and observation by the Professor of Military Science.
- Your degree of demonstrated motivation toward an Army career.

To apply for a three- or two-year Army ROTC scholarship, contact the Professor of Military Science (PMS) at the college or university at which you are currently enrolled or have been accepted.

The Army also offers three- and two-year ROTC scholarships for active-duty enlisted personnel who have completed one or two years of college or have equivalent credit. Applicants must have at least three years (for a three-year scholarship) or two years (for a two-year scholarship) remaining in an approved baccalaureate-degree program.

If you are enlisted and wish to apply for a three- or two-year scholarship, you must:

- Meet the same citizenship, age, and physical requirements as for a four-year scholarship.
- Have completed at least one year of active duty and be eligible for discharge prior to the opening enrollment date of the college or university you plan to attend.
- Be accepted as an academic sophomore (for a three-year scholarship) or an academic junior (for a two-year scholarship) at a college or university offering Army ROTC.
- Have a cumulative grade point average of 2.0 on all previous college work.
- Be under twenty-five years old on June 30 of the calendar year in which you will graduate and be eligible to receive your commission. However, extensions of one year may be granted (up to a total of four) for each year of active duty you have served (e.g., with two years' active service you must be under twenty-seven at the time of appointment).
- Have a GT score of 115 or higher.
- Pass the Army Physical Readiness Test.

If you are awarded one of these scholarships, you are discharged from active duty. You are then required to enlist immediately in the US Army Reserve and to complete an ROTC financial (scholarship) contract. Three- and two-year Army ROTC scholarships for active-duty enlisted personnel are awarded on the following criteria:

- Academic achievement or equivalent credit.
- Leadership potential.
- Demonstrated motivation toward an Army career.
- The recommendation of your Commanding Officer.

To apply for one of these scholarships, write for an application between December 15 and March 15 to: Army ROTC scholarships (AD), Fort Monroe, VA 23651-5000.

If you are an outstanding student or a Reservist who has success-fully completed two years of college, you may be eligible for a two-year Reserve Forces Duty scholarship. To qualify you must:

- Meet the same citizenship, age, and physical requirements as for a four-year scholarship.
- Be enrolled or accepted as a full-time academic junior in any major course of study leading to a baccalaureate degree (except theology) beginning in the fall of the year in which the scholar-ship is awarded.
- Have an academic grade point average of at least 2.7 on a 4.0 scale.
- Pass the Physical Aptitude Examination (if you are a student) or the Army Physical Readiness Test (if you are a Reservist).

If you are awarded a two-year Reserve Forces Duty scholarship, you are required to enlist in the Army National Guard or the US Army Reserve for a period of eight years. If you are already in the Guard or Reserve, you must have at least six years of military service remaining when you enroll in the ROTC advanced course. If you have less than four years remaining and wish to apply for a scholarship, you may extend your enlistment to meet the requirements.

If you are presently a member of the Army National Guard or the US Army Reserve, you should contact your Unit Commander. Students on campus should contact their Professor of Military Science.

The information presented in this section applies to ROTC schol-arship cadets. However, the great majority of ROTC cadets never receive any type of scholarship. Less than 20 percent of ROTC cadets are under scholarship at any given time. All cadets, whether scholarship or nonscholarship, receive the same training and study the same subjects. Eligibility requirements for nonscholarship cadets are generally the same as for scholarship cadets regarding age, moral character, academic performance, physical and medical standards, and absence of criminal acts. It should also be noted that each cadet is judged individually upon his application to join the ROTC program. Applicants who appear to be well motivated for an Army career may have certain requirements waived under special circumstances. The Army, as well as the other services, is primarily interested in the potential value of the cadet to serve in the Army; judgments about an individual's suitability to enter the ROTC pro-gram are certainly based on past performance, but judgments about an individual's potential also play a part in the decision-making process.

Nonscholarship cadets are best advised to contact the Army ROTC detachment at their college or university for the most accurate information about the ROTC program. Incoming freshmen should receive a briefing about ROTC opportunities at the particular institution. Many students choose to take the first two years of the basic course without any intention of entering the advanced course. Almost all colleges and universities give academic credit for ROTC. The best advice for high school students is to look into ROTC before going to college. While still in the junior or senior year in high school, they should contact their high school counselor, local Army recruiter, or the Army ROTC detachment at a nearby college. It is always wise to plan ahead and find out as much as possible about any program before making a decision.

Special Programs

The Army offers a number of special programs in association with its continuing efforts to attract highly qualified people to ROTC. These programs are designed to benefit both the individual and the Army.

Simultaneous Membership Program (SMP)

The Simultaneous Membership Program began in 1979 and offers nonscholarship ROTC cadets the opportunity to serve as officer trainees with an Army National Guard or US Army Reserve unit while working toward a commission. The cadets serve as officer trainees in their Guard or Reserve unit and, under the close supervision of a commissioned officer, perform duties commensurate with those of a Second Lieutenant. To be a member of the SMP, the cadet must be enrolled in the advanced course of ROTC. The program has more than 4,000 cadets participating simultaneously as junior or senior ROTC cadets and members of a Reserve component unit. The student draws the pay of an E-5 Sergeant while serving with the Reserve component in addition to the $100 per month subsistence allowance paid to advanced course cadets. The Army benefits in that the cadet gains additional skills while training with the Guard or Reserve unit. The SMP is somewhat limited by the availability of officer trainee spaces in Reserve component units adjacent to colleges and universities with ROTC programs.

Nursing Program

Commissioning nurses into the Army is the fastest growing aspect of Army ROTC. The program was projected to increase tenfold by school year 1986–87 from its modest beginning in 1982–83, and it is designed to become a major source of Army Nurse Corps (ANC) Lieutenants entering the Army. As with the more traditional ROTC programs, nurses may enter as freshmen, sophomores, or juniors. Those who enroll as juniors must successfully complete basic camp. All cadets attend a nurse summer training program or a traditional advanced camp. As the program expanded and matured, more emphasis was to be placed on the four-year program. A number of scholarships are dedicated to the nursing program and may be awarded to high school students upon graduation or to students already in college. ROTC nursing students incur an eight-year obligation. This commitment may be fulfilled by serving on active duty, with a Reserve component, or a combination of the two. Many nurses enjoy the professional rewards of Army nursing and make it a career. More than 320 colleges and universities that offer Bachelor of Science degrees in nursing are affiliated with ROTC. Upon receiving their degree, passing required state board examinations, and receiving their commission, ROTC nursing graduates take the Officer Basic Course and are then assigned to health care facilities around the country. A total of 42 ROTC nursing commissions were awarded in 1982–83, 112 in 1983–84, and 200 in 1984–85.

DASE-ROTC CO-OP

The requirement for more scientists and engineers, both to serve in the Army and work in civilian capacities, is being partly met through the Department of the Army Scientific and Engineering Reserve Officers Training Corps Cooperative Program (DASE-ROTC CO-OP). Through this program, students work toward a degree in their chosen field and a commission as a Second Lieutenant through ROTC. The unique feature of the program is that the student also works with an Army agency both to improve job skills and to earn funds to help finance the cost of an education. Those who complete all requirements upon graduation and commissioning earn civil service status. Graduates who enter the Regular Army, upon satisfying their active-duty requirement, are eligible to return to the agency for which they worked as a co-op student. Graduates who join either the Army National Guard or the US Army Reserve upon commissioning are normally employed by the agency that sponsored the co-op training or another Army laboratory or facility. This innovative program was being tested in the eastern United States, although employment opportunities are available all over the nation.

Technical Enrichment Program (TEP)

Another method the Army is using to meet its accelerating need for highly skilled scientists and engineers is the Technical Enrichment Program. In fiscal year 1985, thirty ROTC graduates took part in this full-time, Army-funded program for study at the master's degree level. Fields of study include robotics, artificial intelligence, computer-related cognitive science, composite materials (ceramics), human factors engineering, biotechnology, vertical life technology, physics, metallurgy, computer engineering, space systems engineering/operations, and other high-tech and space-related subjects. To be eligible for the program, candidates must have an undergraduate degree that will support master's-level study, be a recent four-year college graduate, and be highly recommended by the chain of command. Upon completing the program, the participants follow a single-track career progression with successive assignments in areas where their academic skills can be of maximum benefit to the Army.

Battalion staff at awards ceremony.

It is probable that the Army will continue to develop programs to attract top-quality students to ROTC. The relatively new G.I. bill and the New Army College Fund can be used in conjunction with ROTC if certain conditions are met.

Curriculum

The Army has made great strides in the past five years in standardizing and improving its curriculum. With minor exceptions, the curriculum for ROTC students is the same no matter what college or university is attended. Campus instruction is based on Military Qualification Standards (MQS), a system designed to establish what officers and future officers must know and do to meet job-related standards and to provide the means for them to meet those standards. MQS programs provide career development information in the primary areas of military skills, professional knowledge, and professional military education. At the precommissioning level, termed MQS I, subject matter is common to all cadets. Once the cadet is commissioned, training becomes increasingly branch-oriented as the officer progresses in rank and responsibility.

MQS I qualification is a continuous process that the Professor of Military Science must use to ensure that all cadets who complete the ROTC program have met the training standards established in the MQS I program. That qualification is the sum of demonstrated performance in military tasks, skills, and knowledge subjects, as well as the result of leadership potential evaluation. Certification on MQS I is through the act of commissioning. To be certified, a cadet must qualify on all MQS I military tasks, skills, and knowledge subjects according to the standards prescribed in the program. Qualification takes place in the classroom, during drill periods, during field training exercises, and at the camps.

MQS I-level military skills are the basic soldiering skills that must be developed before attendance at an Officer Basic Course (OBC). The 64 such skills are grouped into the following areas:

Leadership
Written and Oral
    Communications
Operations and Tactics
Land Navigation
Military Justice
Preventive Medicine and First
    Aid

Physical Readiness
Weapons
Army Training Management
Radio and Wire
    Communication
Nuclear, Biological and
    Chemical (NBC)
    Defense Training
International Law

The military knowledge component of MQS I comprises a group of subjects that describe, in fundamental terms, what the United States Army does and how it goes about doing it. Covered are 20 specific subjects:

Leadership
Principles of War
Ethics and Professionalism
Customs and Traditions of the
 Service
Branches of the US Army
The Law of War
Role of US Army
Role of US Army Reserve
Role of Army National Guard
Organization of US Army
Military History

Military Justice
Command and Staff Functions
Soviet Army
Role of the Noncommissioned
 Officer
US Army Personnel
 Management System
US Army Training Management
US Army Logistics Systems
Post and Installation Support
Intelligence and Combat
 Information

The second MQS I element is the professional military education requirement. It consists of two parts, a baccalaureate degree and undergraduate courses in five designated fields of study. At least one course must be taken in each of three areas: written communications, military history, and human behavior. Though not required, courses in national security policy and management are also recommended. Courses in the written communications category might include Advanced English Composition, Creative Writing, Business Writing, Scientific Writing and Language, Writing for Mass Communications, Linguistics, and Logic. Courses for military history include History of War, American Military History, American Military Affairs, European Military History, History of US Foreign Policy in the Twentieth Century, Advanced History or a Military History course offered by the ROTC detachment that may meet this requirement. Many ROTC detachments have arranged with their universities to have the History Department teach the Military History course for the ROTC Department. Human behavior courses are General Psychology, Sociology, Anthropology, and Ethics. Management courses are Management Science, Decision-making, Industrial Management, Analytical Testing for Decision-making, Management Information Systems, Probability and Statistics, and General Accounting. National security studies include: National Strategy, National Security Affairs, National Defense, International Relations, American Foreign Policy, the Cold War, Economics of

War and Peace, Geopolitics, Comparative Economic Systems, and International Economics.

Fulfilling this requirement usually does not involve any additional course work. The great majority of academic majors, whether in soft skills or hard technical subjects, include courses in all these areas. Educational advisers on the ROTC staff consult closely with each cadet and write out a schedule of classes to insure that all ROTC requirements are fulfilled along with degree requirements.

Basic course cadets (freshmen and sophomores called MS I and MS II cadets) must receive a minimum of 90 military core contact hours. Of the 90 hours, 30 hours (usually accomplished by having cadets meet 1 hour each week) must be accumulated during MS I, with the remaining 60 hours (usually accomplished by having cadets meet 2 hours each week) accumulated during MS II. Military core contact hours accumulated in excess of the minimum in one MS level cannot be applied toward the next MS-level requirements. Advanced course cadets (juniors and seniors called MS III and MS IV cadets) must receive a minimum of 60 military core contact hours for each level of the advanced course (MS III and MS IV). This number of hours is the minimum requirement; in reality, most programs on campus exceed the minimum.

Every Lieutenant who earns a commission through Army ROTC spends part of at least one summer at a camp learning the fundamentals of leadership in a field environment. Many ROTC cadets attend more than one of a wide variety of training opportunities that challenge them both physically and mentally while building upon the skills learned in the classroom.

Basic camp is designed as the entry point into ROTC for college students who did not take part in the program during the first two years of college. Attending basic camp involves no obligation to continue with the ROTC program, though most of those who do attend camp choose to enter the advanced ROTC course. Students who meet requirements and attend basic camp spend six weeks, in a pay status, learning the fundamentals of being a soldier. Offered at Fort Knox, Kentucky, basic camp provides a firsthand sample of Army life. Emphasis is on physical conditioning. Courses include marksmanship, adapting to field conditions, drill and ceremonies, weapons familiarization, first aid, individual tactical training techniques, fire and maneuver, military courtesies, customs and traditions, and the role of the Army.

ROTC advanced camp is the keystone of the summer program and is required for all cadets except those who choose the nurse summer training program or are accepted for Ranger training. Cadets are in a pay status while attending the six-week training camp. Advanced camp usually takes place between a student's junior and senior years at Fort Bragg, North Carolina; Fort Riley, Kansas; or Fort Lewis, Washington. Emphasis is on leadership training with a good sampling of tactical and technical courses and physical conditioning. Advanced camp also serves as a forum in which the cadet's skills and leadership abilities can be evaluated by the Army cadre. It is a physically demanding course with emphasis on small unit tactics, conducting small unit operations, weapons and equipment familiarization, teamwork, and leadership. Advanced camp is one of the most important phases of the ROTC cadet's entire training program.

A select group of cadets each year is chosen to attend Ranger training in lieu of advanced camp. Only the best qualified are sent to Ranger training, at Fort Benning, Georgia, as it is among the most demanding offered by the Army. Graduates are awarded the Ranger tab, which testifies to their superior physical and leadership qualifications and certifies their being among the best-qualified small unit leaders in the world.

Each year a number of cadets supplement the skills learned at advanced camp by attending an additional course during the summer. Airborne training at Fort Benning or Fort Bragg, either before or after advanced camp, is one way the cadet can enrich his summer program. Others attend air assault training at Fort Campbell, Kentucky; Fort Hood, Texas; Fort Rucker, Alabama; or Schofield Barracks, Hawaii. Still others go to Alaska for northern warfare training. A select group learn the fundamentals of helicopter flying during four weeks at Fort Rucker; cadets who attend this program may progress up to their first solo flight. The final enrichment course, the Cadet Troop Leader Training (CTLT) program, offers the opportunity to serve as an "acting Lieutenant" with the Regular Army, the Army National Guard, or the US Army Reserve. Summer training is a key aspect of the cadet's well-rounded military education and is, at the same time, both challenging and rewarding.

Quality is a word often heard in the Army, and nowhere is it more important than in the selection of young men and women who will be commissioned to be leaders in time of peace and, if need be, in war. A tool that the Professors of Military Science use to determine leadership potential and military service suitability is the Precommissioning Assessment System (PAS). The PAS provides a method to determine a student's motivation to serve in a leadership position and to measure a student's potential. By using the PAS, the PMS knows who are the high-potential cadets and also how to design both physical and leadership development programs for those who need them. Equally important, the PAS enables the Professor of Military Science to insure that only the best-qualified cadets earn commissions.

The PAS consists of five components designed to assess critical characteristics in cadets. It assesses motivation through use of a structured interview (SI); mental readiness through the requirement that cadets have at least a 2.0 grade average; medical fitness through medical examinations specified by Army regulations; physical trainability by means of the Physical Aptitude Examination and the Army Physical Readiness Test; and leadership potential through PMS evaluation and use of the Leadership Assessment Program (LAP). The LAP consists of five job-based simulations that measure the individual's performance in administration, counseling, oral presentation, group discussion, and scheduling exercises.

Still another innovation to test and measure a cadet's ability, with a feedback mechanism to point out ways for improvement, is the ROTC achievement testing program, which began in school year 1983–84. This testing program was phased in over three years using such tools as the Nelson-Denny Reading Test, the Missouri College English Test, the Officer Selection Battery, and a review of SAT/ACT results when available. An on-campus mathematics component was to be added later.

ROTC instruction is a matter of interest to the academic community as well as the Army. Many valuable recommendations have been offered through the years by the Army Advisory Panel on ROTC affairs, which consists of distinguished educators and prominent citizens. Included on the panel are representatives of the American Council on Education, the Association of American Colleges, the National Association of State Universities and Land Grant Colleges, the Association of American Universities, the Association of Military Colleges and Schools, and the American Association of State Colleges and Universities.

ROTC Campus Activities

The value that a person derives from an activity is directly proportional to the time and effort he puts into it. Army ROTC encompasses four years of college and attendance at a summer camp. During these periods, there are many opportunities to make lasting friendships and to acquire new interests through ROTC campus activities. Both men and women cadets find that the shared interest of participating in ROTC provides a basis for lasting relationships and an excellent way to meet people. Among ROTC organizations are the Pershing Rifles, Scabbard and Blade, the Society of American Military Engineers, and ROTC companies of the Association of the US Army.

The Pershing Rifles was founded in 1891 at the University of Nebraska; today, companies are organized at many of the colleges and universities having ROTC units. The mission of each company is to achieve a high proficiency in close order drill, military operations, and military bearing and courtesy; to instill discipline and a high sense of honor; to promote strong bonds of friendship among members of the company, and to develop to the maximum degree the characteristics that contribute to the making of better officers and citizens. Members meet monthly and participate in a variety of social activities.

Scabbard and Blade was founded at the University of Wisconsin in 1904. It is an advanced course national honor fraternity with chapters at many colleges and universities having ROTC programs. Membership is by election only and is divided into four classifications; active, alumni, associate, and honorary. Active members are chosen from outstanding cadet officers of the advanced course of the Army, Navy, and Air Force ROTC. The purposes of Scabbard and Blade are to raise the standard of military education in American colleges and universities, to unite in closer relationship their military departments, to encourage and foster the essential qualities of good and efficient officers, and to promote friendship and good fellowship among cadet officers. The cadet elected to Scabbard and Blade must be "an officer and a gentleman." Merit is the sole basis of membership.

The Society of American Military Engineers is a group that promotes the national engineering potential for defense. ROTC companies of the Association of the US Army provide professional exchanges between cadets and military and civic leaders.

All ROTC units offer instruction in some type of adventure training activities such as mountaineering, rappelling, river rafting, and orienteering. Most ROTC detachments furnish color guards for parades, sporting events, holiday observances, graduation and commencement ceremonies, and county fairs. Many detachments participate in sporting events such as 5k or 10k runs, bicycling, and mountain climbing. ROTC cadets frequently participate in community service activities associated with social work and civic projects. These activities not only serve to bring the cadets closer together, but they also help spread the word about ROTC and insure good relations with the academic and civilian communities. Social activities are an important part of all ROTC programs, and the military staffs make an extra effort to help the cadets adjust to college life.

Assignments and Obligations

Early in the final year of the advanced course, cadets are requested to submit first, second, third, and fourth choices of Army branches in which they would like to be commissioned. Although the immediate needs of the Army are paramount, most cadets are commissioned in one of their first three choices. Special Department of the Army selection boards are convened to examine the files of all applicants. The Department of the Army has a limited number of officers it can commission in each branch, and therefore branch assignments are very competitive. The better a cadet has done in the program, the better his academic performance, overall standing in advanced camp, and PMS' recommendation, the better his chances to be awarded his branch choice.

The vast majority of branch assignments are in combat arms such as Infantry, Armor, and Artillery, but the Army offers a wide selection of branches. Basic branches include Infantry, Adjutant General's Corps, Corps of Engineers, Finance Corps, Quartermaster's Corps, Field Artillery, Air Defense Artillery, Armor, Ordnance Corps, Signal Corps, Chemical Corps, Military Police Corps, Transportation Corps, Military Intelligence, Civil Affairs (only in the US Army Reserve), and Aviation. Special branches include Medical Corps, Army Nurse Corps, Dental Corps, Veterinary Corps, Medical Service Corps, Chaplains, and Judge Advocate General's Corps.

As has been discussed previously, all students must sign a contract before they enter the advanced course. Under this contract the cadet agrees to incur a military service obligation. Scholarship students are required to serve in the military for a period of eight years. This obligation may be fulfilled by serving two to four years on active duty, followed by service in the Army National Guard or Army Reserve, or by serving eight years in the Army National Guard or Army Reserve preceded by a three- to six-month active-duty period. The great majority of scholarship students go on active duty for four years; the Army has invested so much money in their education that it only makes sense for them to serve on active duty.

Nonscholarship graduates may serve three years on active duty and five years in the Reserve forces, or they may be selected to serve on Reserve Forces Duty (RFD). If RFD is selected, graduates serve from three to six months on active duty attending an Officer Basic Course, and spend the remainder of their eight-year obligation in the Reserve Forces. Not enough active-duty slots are authorized in the grade of Second Lieutenant to allow all ROTC graduates to go on active duty. No guarantee is offered to ROTC cadets that they will be accepted for active duty. It is a competitive process. The best advice for ROTC cadets is to do as well as they can in all phases of their college career and ROTC training because it opens many more options for them in their career choices. The ROTC student should make efforts early in the program to talk with the Army cadre about career options and what is best for his or her individual career. As US forces are deployed on a worldwide basis, the newly commissioned ROTC graduate may be assigned anywhere in the world. Most of the officers entering the Army for a four-year period are assigned outside of the United States sometime during that period. The ROTC student should make every effort to talk to the ROTC staff members and make known his preference of assignments.

Chapter **V**

The Air Force ROTC Program

Overview

Air Force ROTC is open to all persons who are full-time students at one of the 150 colleges and universities hosting an Air Force ROTC unit, or at one of the 591 institutions that have a cross-town agreement or consortium agreement with an Air Force ROTC host institution.

Successful completion of the Air Force four-year or two-year program and the requirements for an undergraduate degree qualify a person for an Air Force commission. Credit for a portion of the first two years of the four-year program may be granted for completion of two or more years of Junior ROTC, participation in Civil Air Patrol, military school training, or prior United States military service.

Sixty-five hundred Air Force ROTC scholarships are available to qualified students in the four-year and the two-year programs. Each scholarship provides full tuition, laboratory and incidental fees, and reimbursement for curriculum-required textbooks. In addition, a subsistence allowance is paid to students enrolled in the Professional Officer Course (junior and senior years). Scholarships for four, three and one half, and two years are available to all students; however, emphasis is placed on scientific and technical degree fields. Three- and two-year scholarships are available in certain health profession fields. Limited numbers of two-year scholarships are available to students enrolled in nontechnical and nursing fields. The application deadline for four-year scholarships is December 15 prior to the fall term of the school year in which the student wishes to enter college. About 1,500 high school seniors are offered four-year scholarships each year. Application booklets may be obtained from Air Force ROTC, Maxwell Air Force Base, AL 36112. Applicants for three- and two-year scholarships should contact the Professor of Aerospace Studies at any institution having an Air Force ROTC unit. Air Force ROTC enrollment is limited to cadets capable of completing all requirements for a commission before reaching a certain age: under 25 for scholarship recipients (except for prior service personnel, who may be 29); 26½ for flight trainees, and 30 for missile, scientific, or nontechnical specialists. Under certain circumstances, waivers may be granted for students in the last group.

Registration in the four-year program is accomplished in the same manner and at the same time that students enroll in other college courses. Except for students who have been offered and have accepted Air Force ROTC scholarships, no military obligation is involved for students enrolling in Air Force ROTC courses during the freshman and sophomore years.

After completing the first two years of the program, the General Military Course, students compete for entry into the Professional Officer Course. This is normally taken during the junior and senior years. Selection for the Professional Officer Course is highly competitive, based on quality index scores consisting of several weighted factors.

The two-year program consists of only the Professional Officer Course. The academic hours and content of this program and the last two years of the four-year program are identical. To enter the two-year program, a student must have two academic years remaining at either the undergraduate or graduate level, or a combination of the two.

When cadets in the four-year program and applicants for the two-year program enroll in the Professional Officer Course, they also enlist in the Air Force Reserve, which entitles them to $100 a month in nontaxable allowances during the school year. In addition, they agree to accept an Air Force commission, if offered, after successful completion of the program and to serve on active duty for a specified period. Those who enter nonflying career fields agree to serve four years on active duty. Officers accepted for navigation flight training agree to serve for not less than five years after receiving an aeronautical rating. The active-duty commitment for pilots is seven years after completion of flight training.

Men and women students qualified as pilot candidates, except those who already hold a private pilot certificate, participate in a flight instructor program. This program is conducted by a civilian flying service, which reports to the Air Force on the student's motivation and aptitude for flying. The Air Force pays for all instruction.

Women cadets may be assigned to the same career fields as men, including pilot, navigator, and missile officer.

Four-year program cadets normally complete a four-week Air Force ROTC field training course at an Air Force base during the summer before entering the Professional Officer Course (usually after completion of the sophomore year). Students applying for the two-year program receive six weeks of field training; the additional two weeks are devoted to the academic subjects taken on campus in the General Military Course by four-year program cadets. Uniforms, lodging, meals, and travel expenses to and from the field training location are provided by the Air Force. In addition, cadets are paid approximately $350 for the four-week encampment and about $525 for the six-week encampment. In most cases, field training is the student's first exposure to a working Air Force environment and to using junior officer training and leadership techniques. During this time, the Air Force evaluates each student's potential as an officer.

Another on-base summer training program available to Air Force cadets is voluntary. It provides specialized career orientation, with an opportunity to experience leadership, human relations, and management challenges encountered by Air Force junior officers. Up to 1,200 cadets may be selected for either a two- or three-week period and work on an Air Force base between their junior and senior years. Cadets are paid about $184 for the two-week period and about $295 for the three-week period. The Air Force provides meals and lodging during the training period and transportation to and from the training site.

A limited number of cadets may volunteer for the Army's airborne training program. This three-week program is conducted at Fort Benning, GA. Like all other Air Force ROTC programs, this is available to both men and women.

Further details about the Air Force ROTC program may be obtained by writing Air Force ROTC/PA, Maxwell Air Force Base, AL 36112.

Mission

As discussed earlier, Congress passed the National Defense Act of 1947 creating the United States Air Force as a separate service, and with it the Air Force ROTC program. Almost forty years have passed since the beginning of Air Force ROTC, but its mission has remained basically the same: to recruit, educate, and commission highly qualified officers to satisfy stated Air Force requirements.

Although flying is the primary mission of the Air Force, with the basic objective of gaining and maintaining control of the aerospace environment, it is not the only job to be done. Today when science and technology are so much a part of national defense, the Air Force needs the best scientists and engineers the nation can produce. It also needs other professional officers, both men and women, with wide ranges of knowledge and skill. Many young officers who enter the Air Force today do not expect to be pilots or astronauts. They want to be part of the gigantic research and development program or the vast support organization that will keep our country strong and progressive.

In addition to the continuing need for flying personnel, there will always be a need for scientific, engineering, and medical specialists (health profession), as well as management personnel. In the years ahead, Air Force ROTC will continue to concentrate on preparing men and women to assume positions of ever-increasing responsibility and importance in the modern Air Force. The Air Force looks to its ROTC units to provide full-time career officers for the highly specialized fields that are developing as weapons systems become more complex and as the exploration of space progresses.

Organization and Administration

As noted earlier, Congress passed the National Defense Act of 1947 that established the Air Force as a separate service. After World War II, General Dwight D. Eisenhower as Chief of Staff of the War Department had signed General Order No. 124, which established Air Service ROTC units at 78 colleges and universities throughout the nation. In 1952, Air University at Maxwell Air Force Base in Alabama assumed responsibility for the ROTC program, which at that time conducted a four-year program at 188 academic institutions. A new two-year senior program, scholarships, and a junior program were authorized by the ROTC Vitalization Act of 1964. An experimental program to commission women through Air Force ROTC was conducted from 1956 to 1960. Women were again enrolled in the senior program starting in 1969 and in the junior program four years later. Eligible Air Force enlisted men and women pursuing a college degree who are interested in an officer's commission are given an opportunity through competition in the Air Force ROTC Airman Scholarship and Commissioning Program, established in 1973.

Organizationally, Air Training Command assumed command responsibility for the Air University in 1978. In 1979 the Air Force geographic areas were reduced from six to five. In 1983 the Air Force ROTC was separated from Air University, which was designated as a major command, and placed directly under the Air Training Command. Today the ROTC program is directed from Headquarters Air Force ROTC at Maxwell Air Force Base. Headquarters Air Force ROTC is a part of Air Training Command, which is also located at Maxwell. In the continental United States, Air Force ROTC is administratively divided into five geographical areas: the Western Area, headquartered at Mather Air Force Base, Sacramento, California; the Northeast Region, headquartered at McGuire Air Force Base, New Jersey; the Southeast Region, headquartered at Maxwell Air Force Base, Alabama; the Ohio Valley Region, headquartered in Columbus, Ohio; and the Midwest Region, headquartered at Bergstrom Air Force Base, Austin, Texas. The European Region works primarily with junior Air Force ROTC programs at Department of Defense high schools for US military dependents in Europe.

The regional headquarters monitor the efforts of the Air Force ROTC detachments within their jurisdiction and provide assistance as required. Headquarters Air Force ROTC provides policy guidance and direction to the individual detachments while keeping the Region Commanders informed of all policies. The detachment commander, usually a Colonel or Lieutenant Colonel, is also a member of the faculty of the institution and carries the title of Professor of Aerospace Studies. The detachment is composed of active-duty Air Force officers, noncommissioned officers, and civilians.

All Air Force ROTC cadets at an institution are members of the Corps of Cadets. The organization of the Cadet Corps conforms to Air Force structure, with levels of organization ranging from the squad to the air division. A squad has seven to twelve cadets; a flight, two or more squads; a squadron, two or more flights; a group, two or more squadrons; a wing, two or more groups; and an air division, two or more wings. No Cadet Corps is organized lower than squadron level or higher than that indicated by its numerical strength. The numerical strength of the squadron may be 1 to 100; of the group, 101 to 400; of the wing, 401 to 1,600; and of the air division, 1601 and above.

The Cadet Corps provides opportunities for the cadets to assume positions of leadership. A formal system of command is set up, with cadet ranks assigned commensurate with the responsibilities of the position. In this way, cadets not only have a say in their activities and training, but also receive valuable hands-on leadership experience with their peers. Cadets are rotated in command and staff assignments to insure equitable leadership development opportunities. Each cadet officer is afforded the opportunity to occupy at least one command and one staff position while enrolled in the advanced course. Cadets are also able to exercise their learned leadership skills during the encampment. Administratively, the entire program is set up to proceed from basic introductory skills to more complex skills. In leadership training, the cadets must learn first to be good followers and then to be good leaders.

Air Force Junior ROTC

The Air Force Junior ROTC program explores the civilian, industrial, and military aspects of aerospace and teaches students self-reliance, self-discipline, and the characteristics of good leaders. The curriculum integrates social studies and physical sciences through the application to aerospace of five areas of instruction: aviation, national defense, aerospace careers, space, and leadership. The Junior ROTC program was started nationwide in 1966 and has shown steady growth ever since. Today there are 286 Junior ROTC units with an enrollment of approximately 40,000 high school students, of whom about 33 percent are women.

Leadership training is an important aspect of the Air Force Junior ROTC program. In the classroom, cadets study and discuss such subjects as human relations and management and communicative skills to prepare themselves for leadership in any civilian or military field. Cadets also learn military customs and courtesies, flag etiquette, and basic drill positions, movements, and commands that will allow them to participate in parades and ceremonies.

Extracurricular activities of cadets in the Air Force Junior ROTC program are varied and interesting. Some units have drill teams or color guards. Most units offer field trips to Air Force bases, airports, aerospace industries, Federal Aviation Administration and Weather Bureau offices, and other areas related to aerospace education.

Instructors at Air Force Junior ROTC units are retired Air Force commissioned and noncommissioned officers who have been retired for four years or less. They act as fulltime members of the high school faculty and are employed by the local school board.

Air Force Junior ROTC carries no military obligation. Tangible benefits are granted to students who enroll. Students who complete two years of the program may have one term of the Air Force senior ROTC program waived, and students who complete the entire three-year program receive credit for a full year of Air Force ROTC. The principal of the high school having a junior unit may nominate up to five qualified graduating cadets to the Air Force Academy as candidates for appointment. Cadets who do not go on to college but enter the military directly after graduation from high school, and have successfully completed the three-year Air Force Junior ROTC program enter the Air Force one pay grade higher than other enlistees.

Enrollment in the Air Force Junior ROTC program is open to all young people who are at least fourteen years of age, physically fit, and citizens of the United States. For additional information on the Air Force Junior ROTC programs, contact the Public Affairs Office, Air Force ROTC, Maxwell Air Force Base, Alabama 36112.

Scholarships

Air Force ROTC scholarships are available to qualified applicants in both the four- and two-year programs; scholarships are awarded for four, three and a half, three, two and a half, and two years. Each scholarship provides full tuition, laboratory and incidental fees, and full reimbursement for curriculum-required textbooks. In addition, scholarship cadets receive a nontaxable $100 subsistence each month during the school year up to $1,000. This subsistence does not begin until enlistment in the Air Force Reserve and enrollment in the AFROTC college scholarship program.

Competitive four-year scholarships are available primarily to high school seniors who pursue specific scientific degrees (engineering, mathematics, physics, etc.); limited numbers of scholarships are available to those who enroll in certain nontechnical degree programs (business administration, accounting, history, economics, etc.). Four-year scholarships may be extended to four and a half or five years for those in certain academic majors and programs. The Professor of Aerospace Studies at the college where you enroll in Air Force ROTC will evaluate your academic plan and your performance as a cadet and a student, and recommend approval of additional terms of scholarship aid if warranted. If you are designated a scholarship winner, the Air Force pays for travel from your home to the Air Force ROTC unit at the college you have selected.

Room and board are not paid by any ROTC program. The scholarship award is based on individual merit, not on financial aid.

Four-year scholarship applications are contained in the Air Force ROTC Four-Year College Scholarship Application Booklet. The booklet may be obtained from a high school counselor, an Air Force admissions counselor, the Professor of Aerospace Studies at a college offering Air Force ROTC, or from AFROTC/RROO, Maxwell Air Force Base, Alabama 36112. The deadline for submitting applications is December 15 to compete for the next year's fall semester. Early submission is encouraged. Selection boards convene in November, January, and March. Applicants who are not selected by a board and are not disqualified from further consideration are considered automatically by a subsequent board.

Applicants for four-year scholarships are evaluated on the following criteria:

- Scholastic Aptitude Test (SAT) or American College Test (ACT). (The SAT and ACT must be taken by December. Registration for the ACT and SAT closes four to six weeks prior to the test date. Minimum SAT scores to qualify are a total score of 1000 with math score of 500 and verbal score of 450.)
- High school academic record (high school grade point average must be at least 2.5 on a 4.0 point scale).
- Recommendation from a high school officer. (High school standing must be in top 25 percent. Minimum GPA and class standing must be achieved at the end of the junior year.)
- Record of extracurricular activities. (Generally speaking, the more extracurricular activities the applicant is involved in, the better his chances for a scholarship. Particularly helpful is involvement as an officer or leader or organizations).
- Personal interview by a representative of Air Force ROTC.

All scholarship recipients must pass a medical examination and be accepted at a college or university that offers the Air Force ROTC four-year program. A list of schools offering that program is given in the Appendix. You must be sure that the schools to which you apply offer the academic major(s) you indicate on your scholarship application. In addition, you must apply to be admitted in those academic areas. For example, if you are awarded a scholarship as an engineering major, you must attend a school affiliated with Air Force ROTC in order to use your scholarship. It is advisable to contact the Air Force ROTC unit associated with the college that you will attend to verify that your specific degree is offered.

Each four-year scholarship recipient must sign an agreement with the United States Air Force that provides the following obligations (those under legal age in the state where the college is located must have the agreement signed by a parent or legal guardian):

- Enroll in the academic area in which the scholarship is offered.
- Enlist in the Air Force Reserve and enroll in Air Force ROTC beginning in the fall term.
- Successfully complete one quarter or semester of college instruction in a major Indo-European or Asian language prior to commissioning.
- Satisfactorily complete a four-week summer field training encampment at an Air Force base (normally scheduled between the sophomore and junior years).
- Complete the Air Force ROTC four-year program.
- Accept a commission as an Air Force officer.
- Serve four years on active duty.

Air Force ROTC four-year scholarships are awarded only in the academic majors necessary to meet Air Force needs, which change from year to year. At present, the most scholarships are offered to students in specific engineering disciplines. Other awards are made to students majoring in certain scientific disciplines and in limited nontechnical curricula. Keep these facts in mind when indicating your choice of major. When selecting your college, be sure that it offers the academic major in which your scholarship is awarded. Approximately 80 percent of the four-year scholarships are awarded in fields such as aeronautical engineering, aerospace engineering, architectural engineering, astronautical engineering, civil engineering, industrial engineering, mechanical engineering, metallurgical engineering, nuclear engineering, and systems engineering. About 50 percent of the scholarships are awarded in electrical engineering; 18 percent in science majors such as architecture, computer science, mathematics, meteorology, and physics; and 2 percent in nontechnical majors like accounting, business administration, economics, and management.

The Air Force has certain weight standards that must be met before a student may use a scholarship and while on active duty. If you appear overweight during a scholarship interview, you may be weighed. If you exceed the maximum weight but present an acceptable military appearance, you may request a weight adjustment. Only a military doctor or an Air Force ROTC unit may adjust your maximum allowable weight. The required aerobic run time for men is 12 minutes for 1.5 miles, and for women 14 minutes 24 seconds. This is also an active-duty requirement. Below is the maximum allowable weight chart for men and women:

Height (in inches)	Men	Women
60	153	130
61	155	132
62	158	134
63	160	136
64	164	139
65	169	144
66	174	148
67	179	152
68	184	156
69	189	161
70	194	165
71	199	169
72	205	174
73	211	179
74	218	185
75	224	190
76	230	196
77	236	201
78	242	206
79	248	211
80	254	216

Air Force ROTC four-year scholarship selection boards are composed of senior Air Force officers. The boards evaluate qualified applicants according to officer potential and the whole-person concept. They review high school academic records, college entrance examination results, leadership experience, extracurricular activities, and work experience. Additional information is obtained from a personal interview, a questionnaire, and an evaluation by high school officials. Scholarship boards meet in November, January, and March. Early application is to your advantage, since selection opportunities are generally higher on the earlier boards. Applications of finalists are reviewed by a board after the results of a personal interview reach Air Force Headquarters. Applicants selected by the board to receive a scholarship are notified within 45 days after the board meets. Applicants considered noncompetitive are released from further consideration. Applicants neither selected nor released are considered again by the next selection board.

After the selection boards have evaluated the applications, applicants are ranked in descending order of board scores. The number of selections in each major depends on the needs of the Air Force. The total number of scholarship designees is approximately 3,000. Several hundred alternates are chosen to fill vacancies as designees decline or are otherwise disqualified before the final acceptance date in October of each year. Only alternates who complete a certified medical examination and who enter college and enroll in Air Force ROTC during the current fall term are considered for scholarship entitlements after the start of the fall term. The selection of alternates is based on the needs of the Air Force. If an applicant receives a four-year scholarship after he has already enrolled in a college or university, his tuition fees are refunded.

To apply for a four-year scholarship, you must obtain a Social Security number before submitting your application. SS form 5 is available at district Social Security offices. To receive a four-year scholarship you must:

- Be a citizen of the United States.
- Graduate from high school or hold an equivalent certificate.
- Be at least seventeen years old when accepting scholarship.
- Be under twenty-five years old when completing officer training (prior active-duty military service can extend this date).
- Not be or have been enrolled as a full-time student in a junior college or university except for joint high school/college programs.

Other scholarship opportunities exist, on a competitive basis, for students already enrolled in college. These programs vary slightly each year; interested students should contact the Professor of Aerospace Studies at a college offering Air Force ROTC for current and specific information. Scholarship applications are made directly to the Professor of Aerospace Studies. Scholarship award policies are designed to attract students to fields in which the Air Force needs more officers. Therefore, fields that attract a sufficient number of applicants receive few, if any, scholarships. Current prime examples are pilot candidates (majoring in any academic area) and nontechnical majors. The Air Force needs many people with these interests, but the fields are competitive even without scholarships. If you want to fly or have a nontechnical major, consider becoming a navigator. Scholarships exist for up to the last three and a half years of college for navigator cadets.

The scholarships for three and a half, three, two and a half, and two years are available to students who are pursuing specific scientific/technical degrees (engineering, math, physics, etc.). The following career categories normally are open to these scholarship applicants: navigator, missile launch officer, scientific/technical, and engineering.

Limited numbers of two-year scholarships may be available to students enrolled in certain nontechnical degree programs (business administration, accounting, history, economics, etc.).

Two- and three-year scholarships are available to students pursuing a premedical or preosteopathic (physician) degree regardless of academic major.

Two-year scholarships are available to students pursuing a nursing-related baccalaureate or higher degree from a school of nursing accredited by the National League for Nursing or from certain schools in eight states accredited by the state professional agency recognized by the US Department of Education.

Applicants for Air Force scholarships of less than four years are also selected on the basis of the whole-person concept, which includes both objective (grade point average, etc.) and subjective (interview evaluation, etc.) factors.

The Air Force ROTC Pre-Health Professions Scholarship Program, Airman Scholarship and Commissioning Program, and Nurse Program are discussed under Special Programs later in this chapter.

Qualifications and Requirements

Generally speaking, eligibility requirements and qualifications for Air Force ROTC are more stringent for scholarship cadets than for nonscholarship cadets. Although scholarships attract high-quality students with academic specialties needed by the Air Force, most cadets participate in ROTC without a scholarship. In academic year 1984–85, 7,500 of the approximately 25,000 Air Force ROTC cadets had scholarships.

Cadets not on scholarship are provided with textbooks for ROTC courses and uniforms (usually worn one day a week) at no cost. In addition, they receive a $100 tax-free monthly allowance during their junior and senior years and are paid a salary while attending a summer field training encampment following their sophomore year. Pilot candidates receive flight instruction during the last 24 months of Air Force ROTC to determine their flying aptitude.

As previously noted, the Air Force ROTC program is divided into the General Military Course (freshman and sophomore years) and the Professional Officer Course (junior and senior years). To qualify for the General Military Course, the student must:

- Be a full-time student at a college that offers Air Force ROTC.
- Be a United States citizen (for contract purposes, noncitizens can take ROTC for academic credit, but they cannot be contracted).
- Be in good physical condition.
- Be of good moral character.
- For pilot or navigator, complete commissioning requirements before reaching age 25 as of June 30 in your estimated year of commissioning (unless you have been on active duty).
- For nonscholarship students, fulfill all commissioning requirements prior to age 30 (may be waived for prior service up to age 35, providing the individual can be brought on active duty prior to reaching age 35).
- Be at least 14 years old.
- Be at least 17 years old to receive a scholarship appointment.

Qualifications for the Professional Officer Course are more stringent. In addition to the requirements for the General Military Course, the student must:

- Have two academic years remaining (undergraduate, graduate, or combination of both).
- Qualify on the Air Force physical examination.
- Qualify on the Air Force Officer Qualifying Test.
- Be interviewed and selected by a board of Air Force officers.
- Successfully complete a four-week field training course if in the four-year program. Two-year program applicants must complete a six-week field training course.

No special application procedure applies for nonscholarship cadets in the four-year program. Simply register for Air Force ROTC in the same manner and at the same time you register for your other college courses. To apply for the two-year program, contact the Professor of Aerospace Studies at a university where Air Force ROTC is offered. Your application must be made early in the academic year preceding your last two years of college, normally the sophomore year. You must have two academic years of study as an undergraduate or a graduate student remaining after completing the six-week field training course. For additional information on the Air Force ROTC program at a specific college or university, write to the Professor of Aerospace Studies. A list of schools that offer Air Force ROTC is given in the Appendix.

Special Programs

The Air Force offers a wide variety of special programs to attract and retain personnel with specialized skills needed to meet continuing Air Force requirements. These programs fall into three categories: special scholarships, special educational programs, and special off-campus learning opportunities.

The Air Force Pre-Health Professions Scholarship Program (Pre-HPSP) in selected medical areas is offered to encourage students to earn commissions through Air Force ROTC and go on to acquire doctorates in health career fields. Men and women college students and active-duty Air Force airmen who are pursuing a medical or osteopathic degree are eligible to compete in the Pre-HPSP, which includes awarding of scholarships. Members are commissioned Second Lieutenants in the Air Force on completion of Air Force ROTC and baccalaureate degree requirements.

Additional tuition assistance for graduate-level health schooling expenses is guaranteed under the Armed Forces Health Professions Scholarship Program for Air Force ROTC Pre-HPSP graduates on acceptance at an appropriate graduate-level school. This scholarship sponsors the remaining health professions schooling. Those accepted into health professions schools are transferred to the Medical Service Corps. Graduates who fail to gain health professions school acceptance by the date of graduation enter active duty like any other Air Force ROTC commissionee. Applicants incur an additional active-duty commitment based on the number of years required to complete the health professions school.

In addition to basic requirements for entry into the Professional Officer Course, Pre-HPSP applicants must also meet the following criteria:

- A very high grade point average (which is established annually) in the following basic curriculum:
  One full year (2 semesters, 3 quarters, etc.) of each of the following (either completed or programmed for completion by the end of the junior year): English, general chemistry (including lab), organic chemistry (including chemistry), physics (including lab), general biology or zoology (including lab), and mathematics (equivalent to analytical geometry and differential and integral calculus).
- Three letters of recommendation from science faculty, members of health professions school selection committee or advisory committee, dean of health professions school, or dean of students in the college of current enrollment.
- A personal statement describing the applicant's knowledge and interest in a career as a health profession officer in the appropriate professional field.

The two- and three-year Pre-HPSP scholarships can be in any academic major (biology, zoology, chemistry, etc.).

Airman Scholarship and Commissioning Program

Enlisted members of the Air Force may apply for college scholarships through the Air Force ROTC Airman Scholarship and Commissioning Program (ASCP). The scholarships cover costs of tuition, laboratory and other incidental fees, and books and pay $100 a month tax-free while the cadet is enrolled in Air Force ROTC and pursuing an academic curriculum leading to a degree and Second Lieutenant's commission.

Scholarships for four, three and a half, three, two and a half, and two years are available in a number of fields as described under Qualifications and Requirements. Two selection boards convene annually, in February and July. February board selectees start school in September, and July board selectees the following January. Actual terms of scholarship entitlement are based on planned academic programs and age restrictions.

Scholarship application and eligibility requirements are contained in Air Force Regulation 53-20, The US Air Force Academy Board. Base education offices process applications and can provide the latest information on the program, which culminates in discharge of the airman from active duty, enrollment in Air Force ROTC on campus, and commissioning.

Air Force ROTC Nurse Program

Student nurses pursuing at least a baccalaureate degree at a National League for Nursing–accredited school of nursing or certain state-approved schools of nursing are eligible to enroll in either the four-year or the two-year Air Force ROTC program. They also may compete for two-year scholarships to finance the last two years of college.

Air Force ROTC nurses also compete for entry into the Nurse Supervisor/Internship Program as their initial assignment. They enjoy a marked advantage when competing for USAF-sponsored programs such as nurse anesthetist, flight nurse, midwife, and OB/GYN practitioner as well as for graduate education programs.

Enrollment procedures are the same as for the four-year and two-year programs. Student nurse cadets or applicants must meet the minimum grade point average of at least 2.5 on a 4.0 scale. They must submit a résumé, references, and recommendations. The Professor of Aerospace Studies on campus will assist in securing the recommendations.

Veterans

Honorably discharged veterans who meet the same criteria as other students may enter the four-year program at the start of their junior year. The required four-week summer camp may be taken later in the program. Veterans may qualify for the GI Bill or Veterans Educational Assistance Program (VEAP) in addition to scholarship money, the tax-free allowance, and other financial aid to which they are entitled.

Airman Early Release Program

Active-duty Air Force airmen may be released from active duty for the purpose of enrollment in the Air Force ROTC Professional Officer Course (POC) and ultimately receive a commission. Airmen who can complete degree requirements in no more than two years and are accepted by an institution offering Air Force ROTC may apply for early release following award of an Air Force ROTC enrollment allocation.

Application and eligibility requirements are contained in Air Force Regulation 39-10, Administrative Separation of Airmen. Interested airmen should contact the nearest Air Force ROTC detachment to obtain the latest information. Accepted applicants are eligible for all Air Force ROTC benefits. On completion of Air Force ROTC and degree requirements, cadets are commissioned as Second Lieutenants.

Educational Opportunities and Special Educational Programs

Certain qualified Air Force ROTC cadets may request an educational delay in reporting to active duty in order to complete graduate work or a professional school.

Minuteman Educational Program

Cadets selected for duty as missile launch officers in the Minuteman Missile Program have the opportunity to participate in the Minuteman Educational Program, which can lead to a master's degree. The program pays full tuition, and no additional service commitment is incurred.

Air Force Institute of Technology

Graduate study for officers in master's and doctoral programs may be completed through the Air Force Institute of Technology (AFIT). Outstanding Air Force ROTC graduates majoring in engineering, scientific, and technical fields may enter through the AFIT special program.

Basic Meteorology Program

Air Force ROTC cadets who wish to serve as weather officers with the Air Weather Service but are not majoring in meteorology may apply for the Basic Meteorology Program. Applicants must complete six semester hours of college mathematics through integral calculus and six hours of physics with laboratory and maintain an overall 2.0 GPA on a 4.0 scale. Cadets should apply to the Professor of Aerospace Studies for selection by the Air Force Institute of Technology for initial assignment of 49 weeks of specialized instruction at a civilian institution. Basic Meteorology Program students receive full pay and allowances while attending school. Although the program is a nondegree program, students receive academic credit and some schools award a bachelor's degree in meteorology. Students incur no additional service commitment.

Dietitian Internship

During the senior year of Air Force ROTC, cadets seeking entrance to Hospital General Dietetic Internship programs approved by the American Dietetic Association may apply directly to Headquarters AFMPC/Surgeon General for direct entry into the internship as their initial active-duty assignment. Applicants should have a course emphasis that meets academic requirements for dietetic internship. Although selection is not guaranteed, Air Force cadets enjoy a distinct advantage since the Air Force ROTC provides the greatest member of selectees in the program.

Graduate Law

First- and second-year graduate law students may apply for and enter the Air Force ROTC two-year program. Headquarters USAF/Judge Advocate guarantees that they will serve as a Judge Advocate if all ROTC academics and bar requirements are met following enlistment in the Professional Officer Course. Applicants should contact the Professor of Aerospace Studies for application procedures.

Helicopter Combat Crew Training

All former US military helicopter pilots (including Warrant Officers) enrolled in Air Force ROTC may receive a direct assignment to helicopter combat crew training following commissioning. No age limitation or minimum helicopter pilot time exists. An aeronautical rating board selects qualified volunteers prior to commissioning.

Special Off-Campus Programs

Five Air Force ROTC programs provide specialized off-campus learning experiences for cadets: field training, airborne training, base visits, advanced training, and flight instruction.

Field training is of two types: a four-week course for cadets in the four-year program and a six-week course for two-year program students. Students in the four-year program normally attend field training between their sophomore and junior years. Two-year applicants must attend field training before entering the Professional Officers Course. Field training is hosted each summer by several Air Force installations.

Field training is designed to stimulate the development of military leadership. This is accomplished through the curriculum and associated activities. The curriculum consists of aircraft, aircrew, career, and survival orientation, junior officer training, physical training, small arms training, supplemental training and human relations education, and equal opportunity training. The six-week program has an additional 60 hours of academics, which are similar to the 60 hours of on-campus academics taken by the four-year program cadets in the freshman and sophomore years. Students receive pay and allowances authorized by current directives at the time of field training attendance.

Selected Air Force ROTC cadets may attend airborne training as an extracurricular activity. The Army conducts airborne training at Fort Benning, Georgia. On completion of the school, Air Force ROTC cadets may wear the Army "jump wings."

The vast scope of the Air Force is difficult to portray in the classroom. Air Force ROTC cadets may have the opportunity to visit Air Force bases for a firsthand observation of the operating Air Force. These trips are made on weekends or scheduled to coincide with school vacation periods. Cadets may be flown by military aircraft to an Air Force base where they receive facility tours and mission briefings and inspect aircraft and other technical equipment. Each group is accompanied by an Air Force officer/instructor who adds knowledge of the many facets of Air Force missions to the cadets' visual lessons.

Selected cadets may have the opportunity to go to active-duty Air Force bases for a two- or three-week period during the summer following their junior year. As advanced training cadets, they receive specialized career orientation and an opportunity to experience leadership, human relations, and management challenges encountered by Air Force junior officers. Also, cadets become familiar with the Air Force "way of life." Cadets receive pay and allowances authorized by current directives at the time of advanced training attendance.

Air Force ROTC pilot candidates not yet certified as private pilots participate in the Flight Instruction Program (FIP). The program is conducted during the last 24 months of Air Force ROTC and is at Air Force expense. Flying lessons are taken at a Federal Aviation Administration-approved civilian flying school near the campus. The program also includes ground school instruction, usually taught by Air Force pilots or navigators. Ground school includes instruction in meteorology, principles of flight, radio communications, and FAA regulations.

Curriculum

The Air Force ROTC provides preprofessional preparation for future Air Force officers. It is designed to develop men and women who can apply their education to their initial assignments as commissioned officers. Air Force ROTC courses normally are taken for academic credit as part of a student's electives; the amount of credit given toward a degree varies with different colleges and universities. The two major phases of the curriculum are the General Military Course and the Professional Officer Course.

General Military Course

The General Military Course (GMC) is a two-year course normally taken during the freshman and sophomore years. It covers two main themes: the development of air power, and the contemporary Air Force in the context of US military organization.

AS 100 (1 hour a week). Aerospace Studies (AS) 100, the freshman year, usually is the student's first academic exposure to military subjects. Most students begin this study with a discussion of officership. The course focuses on the basic characteristics of air doctrine; US Air Force mission and organization; functions of US strategic offensive and defensive, general purpose, and aerospace support forces; officership; and assessment of written communicative skills. AS 100 also deals with US perceptions of the Soviet threat. The course is open to all students; many students take it without any plans to continue in the ROTC program.

AS 200 (1 hour a week). AS 200 focuses on factors contributing to change in the nature of military conflict; the development of air power from its earliest beginnings through two World Wars; the evolution of air power concepts and doctrines; the role of technology in the growth of air power; a history of air power employment in military and nonmilitary operations in support of national objectives; and an assessment of oral communicative skills. The changing global political situation and its impact on the use of military power are also discussed. Unless the student is on an Air Force ROTC scholarship, no military obligation is incurred by taking AS 200.

Professional Officer Course

The Professional Officer Course (POC) is a two-year course of instruction in aerospace studies, normally taken during the junior and senior years. The curriculum covers Air Force leadership and management and American defense policy.

AS 300 (3 hours a week). AS 300, normally taken in the junior year, is an integrated management course emphasizing the concepts and skills required by the successful manager and leader. The curriculum includes individual motivational and behavioral processes, leadership, communication, and group dynamics, providing the foundation for the development of the junior officer's professional skills. Course material on the fundamentals of management emphasizes decision-making, the use of analytic aids in planning, organizing, and controlling in a changing environment, and evolving professional management concepts. Organizational and personal ethical values, management of change, organizational power, politics, and managerial strategy are discussed within the context of the military organization. Actual Air Force case studies are used throughout the course to enhance the learning and communication process. Group discussions, case studies, and problem-solving are employed as teaching devices. Participation in problem-solving exercises and field trips is a part of the curriculum.

AS 400 (3 hours a week). AS 400, normally taken in the senior year, comprises 90 hours of academic study plus leadership laboratory. The course includes examination of the needs for national security; analysis of the evolution of the American defense strategy and policy; examination of the methods of managing conflict; extensive study of alliances and regional security agreements and commitments by the United States; analysis of arms control and the threat of war; and study of the formulation of American defense policy and strategy. Special topics of interest focus on the military as a profession, officership, and the military justice system. Continued emphasis is given to developing both written and oral communicative skills.

Once students have entered the Professional Officer Course, they are under contract to the Air Force. As discussed earlier, all students have to be accepted by the Professor of Aerospace Studies before they can be enrolled in the POC. The student should be strongly committed to the Air Force before making the decision to enter the course.

Leadership Laboratory. Leadership laboratory is a cadet-centered activity. It is largely cadet-planned and -directed on the premise that it provides leadership training experiences that will improve a cadet's ability to perform as an Air Force officer. The freshman and sophomore leadership laboratory program introduces Air Force customs and courtesies, drill and ceremonies, wearing the uniform, career opportunities in the Air Force, education and training benefits, and the life and work of an Air Force officer. The lab also includes opportunities for field trips to Air Force installations. Initial experiences include preparing the cadets for individual, squadron, and flight movements in drill and ceremonies and for the field training assignment prior to the junior year. All activities are designed to prepare the cadet for successful completion of the Professional Officer Course.

The junior and senior leadership laboratory program involves cadets in advanced leadership experiences to prepare for active duty. Cadet responsibilities include planning, organizing, directing, coordinating, and controlling the activities of the Cadet Corps; preparing briefings and written communications; and providing interviews, guidance, information, and other services that will increase the performance and motivation of all cadets. Within this structure, continued emphasis is given to developing communicative skills. Leadership laboratory provides advanced leadership experiences and preparation for transition from civilian to military life.

The Senior Cadet Officer, the Cadet Commander of the Cadet Corps, is responsible for establishing a plan and operating the program for the leadership laboratory. He is responsible for such activities as rifle teams, drill teams, briefings, and the military ball and for planning, organizing, and conducting parades and ceremonies in coordination with the Army and Navy ROTC units. Air Force officers of the ROTC detachment act as advisors to the Cadet Commander and his staff, and they have final responsibility for the leadership laboratory. However, the officers allow the cadets to take the initiative and make the decisions regarding the operation of the laboratory.

The teaching staff of each Department of Aerospace Studies is composed of well-educated Air Force officers who are selected for their professional experience, academic background, and instructor qualifications. Most have attended at least two Air Force schools in their particular field and have received professional officer education at an Air University school. Completion of the Air University Educational Development Center, an academic instructor course that is the "teacher's college of the Air Force," is required.

In classes conducted in small seminars, cadets engage in group discussions, debates, problem-solving, and simulation activities that require maximum individual participation and group cooperation. This student-centered approach to learning encourages inquiry, logical thinking, the use of imagination, and the practice of sound judgment—all important attributes of a successful Air Force officer.

ROTC Campus Activities

The cadet-operated corps is the basis for the leadership laboratory and a proving ground for the cadets. Many corps-sponsored activities, however, take place outside the laboratory. Among the activities are rifle team, cross-country team, drill teams, cadet bugle corps, cadet flying clubs, cadet newspaper, color guards, and honor guards. Not all Air Force ROTC detachments have all these activities, but all detachments are involved in intramural sports and social activities within the civilian community. All the service ROTC detachments are interested in establishing good relations with both the academic and civilian communities, and participation by cadets in community fund-raising events, parades, and special benefits serves to enhance the image of the military in general and the Air Force in particular.

Air Force ROTC cadets are eligible for membership and participation in the local activities of such national military societies as Pershing Rifles and Scabbard and Blade at institutions having Army or Navy ROTC programs. Some cadets also participate in the Arnold Air Society Squadron and the Angel Flight.

The Arnold Air Society is a professional honorary service organization of Air Force ROTC cadets from the nation's leading colleges and universities. It is a private, tax-exempt, nonprofit organization established to foster good relations among Air Force ROTC, the Air Force, the campus, and the community. It was formed at the University of Cincinnati in 1947, with the approval of the late General H.H. "Hap" Arnold, who was the first Chief of Staff of the Army Air Corps and who was chosen to be the first honorary National Commander. The United States Air Force officially recognized the Society in 1948.

The Angel Flight is an honorary service organization of young women from leading colleges and universities having an Air Force ROTC unit. It is a private, tax-exempt, nonprofit organization sponsored by the Arnold Air Society. The Angel Flight was founded at the University of Omaha in 1952 and was called the Sponsor Corps. The concept spread quickly, and by 1957 the Angel Flight had become a national idea with many activities. It is now recog-

A drill team in action.

nized by the Air Force and receives support from the Air Force Association through Arnold Air Society sponsorship. Its purpose is to further the cause of the Air Force by promoting the interest of college students in the Air Force ROTC program. Angels support the ROTC through activities and programs aimed at publicizing the local detachment and university. Angels assist at social functions, conduct campus tours, and promote Air Force ROTC programs. They help plan and sponsor military functions and participate in military drill teams, parades, and such special events as half-time performances at football and basketball games. They also work with underprivileged groups in various charitable activities.

Assignments and Obligations

Air Force ROTC cadets who successfully complete undergraduate degree requirements and ROTC requirements are commissioned into the Air Force as Second Lieutenants. Unlike the Army, the Air Force guarantees the newly commissioned officer that he or she will go on active duty. The Air Force closely monitors the number of cadets in its Professional Officer Course so that all graduating cadets have an authorized position to fill in the active-duty Air Force upon graduation and commissioning.

Air Force ROTC cadets in the Professional Officer Course who stand in the upper half of their class in military training, in the summer encampment training, and in academic standing are eligible for designation as Distinguished Cadets by the Professor of Aerospace Studies. Normally such a designation is made within 60 days after a cadet enters Aerospace Studies 400; however, the designation may be made as late as the day preceding graduation and commissioning. Because Distinguished Cadets may make advance application for a regular appointment, cadets who indicate a desire to make such an application are usually identified and designated as "distinguished" early enough to enable them to apply 160 days prior to graduation. This program has no quota; the selection emphasizes quality rather than quantity.

Immediately prior to graduation, the Professor of Aerospace Studies officially selects distinguished Air Force ROTC graduates. The letter of designation is usually presented at the commissioning exercises, and the recipient is offered a regular commission as a Second Lieutenant in the Air Force. Other AFROTC graduates are commissioned Second Lieutenants in the US Air Force Reserve and are called to active duty after graduation. The Air Force evaluates the performance of the Reserve Second Lieutenants after their first two years of active duty. If their effectiveness reports are sufficiently high, they may be offered a regular commission in the Air Force.

All Air Force ROTC cadets, whether on scholarship or not, incur at least a four-year active-duty commitment and an inactive reserve commitment to bring the total up to eight years.

- Nonflying officers serve four years' active duty with a four-year inactive reserve commitment. Nonflying officers can serve in a variety of positions: as a missileer with a complex weapons system; as a scientist/engineer in research and development, electronics, communications, computers, etc.; or as support officer in personnel, comptroller, management, education and training, security police, logistics, health professions, and other fields.
- Pilots serve seven years after completion of flying training. Air Force pilot training is a 49-week program conducted at five bases in the United States. Officers must meet the required physical qualifications and apply in time to enter training before reaching 27½ years of age.
- Navigators serve five years after navigator training with a two-year reserve commitment. Navigator training is available to

qualified commissioned officers. The 28-week undergraduate Navigator Training Course is taught at Mather Air Force Base, California. The instruction is divided into academics, flying, and officer training. Upon successful completion of this program, the students continue in specialized training at Mather. Each student's training is tailored to the specific weapon system to which she or he will be assigned. Following completion of specialized training, graduates proceed to advanced flight centers for additional training. Officers must meet physical qualifications and apply in time to enter training prior to reaching 27½ years of age.

- Pre-Health Professions Scholarship Program members normally incur an additional commitment depending on the time required to complete the appropriate health professions school. Graduates who fail to gain entrance into the appropriate health professions school by their graduation date are called to active duty for four years.

- Nurse graduates must agree to accept a commission in the Air Force Nurse Corps. Two consecutive licensing exams are permitted, if required. Nonscholarship nurse cadets who twice fail the licensing exam are afforded the option of requesting active duty as a line officer in lieu of mandatory release. Scholarship nurse cadets who twice fail the licensing exam serve four years as a line officer the same as any other nonflying Air Force ROTC graduate.

Newly commissioned Air Force officers reporting for active duty soon realize that Air Force life has its own customs, its own high standards, and its own special problems, all developing out of the nature of the Air Force mission and the serious responsibility inherent in carrying out that mission. The more the new officer understands the character of his new life and all its facets, the better he will be able to take advantage of and enjoy the opportunities of his Air Force career.

Chapter **VI**

The Navy ROTC Program

Overview

The Navy and the Marine Corps administer a shared ROTC program under the auspices of the Department of the Navy. Although it is a shared program, each service administers its program independently and has the responsibility to insure that its program produces qualified officers to fill its positions. The first two years of the four-year curriculum are common for both Navy and Marine Corps midshipmen; the midshipmen make a choice in their third year for the Navy option or the Marine Corps option. They then take Navy-specific or Marine Corps-specific subjects in their last two years. In this short overview, the two programs are described separately.

Navy ROTC at 65 colleges and universities across the country offers commissions in the Navy to college students who complete either two or four years of Naval Science study on campus. The two programs are called the College Program and the Scholarship Program. The primary objective of the programs is to train officer candidates for eventual appointment in the unrestricted line. In addition to students already enrolled in college programs, qualified enlisted personnel on active duty are eligible to apply for the Navy/Marine Corps ROTC scholarship program.

Four-Year Scholarship Program: students are selected from national competition and are appointed midshipmen, Naval Reserve. They may be granted the compensation and benefits authorized by law during the basic course (not to exceed 20 months) for a total period of not more than four years (40 months). During this period of college, the Navy pays for tuition, fees, and textbooks and provides uniforms and a subsistence allowance of $100 per month.

Two-Year Scholarship Program: students are selected from

national competition of applicants with advanced college standing. They are appointed midshipmen, Naval Reserve, upon reporting for enrollment in the NROTC advanced course. Before starting the advanced course, they must complete a six-week summer course of instruction at the Naval Science Institute, which provides the Naval Science and drill equivalent of the NROTC basic course. Those enrolled in the two-year Scholarship Program have the same privileges and obligations as those in the four-year Scholarship Program.

Four-Year College Program: Students are selected from those applying for enrollment at each NROTC unit. During the first two years in the basic course, students have the status of civilians who have entered into a contract with the Navy. Upon enrollment in the advanced course, College Program students enlist in the Naval Reserve. Upon graduation and completion of Naval Science requirements, students are commissioned as Ensigns in the Naval Reserve. The Navy provides uniforms, Naval Science textbooks, and $100 a month subsistence allowance for a maximum of 20 months during the advanced course. Three-, two-, and one-year scholarships are available to College Program students applying to the Scholarship Program.

Two-Year College Program: Students selected are those with advanced college standing who qualify for enrollment in the advanced course. They must first successfully complete the six-week course at the Naval Science Institute. Those enrolled in the two-year College Program have the same privileges and obligations as those in the four-year College Program.

Information about the College Program is available from any NROTC unit. For more information about the Scholarship Program, contact a Navy or Marine Corps recruiting station, or write to the Commander, Navy Recruiting Command, 4105 Wilson Boulevard, Arlington, VA 22203.

The great majority of Navy/Marine Corps ROTC detachments offer Marine Corps commissions to college students who complete four years of Naval Science study on campus. The two types of programs are called the College Program and the Scholarship Program. In addition to students already enrolled in college programs, qualified enlisted personnel on active duty are eligible to apply for the Navy/Marine Corps ROTC Scholarship Program.

Four-Year Scholarship Program: Students are selected from national competition and are appointed midshipmen Naval Reserve and identified as Marine Corps options. They may be granted the compensation and benefits authorized by law during the basic course (not to exceed 20 months) for a total period of not more than four years (40 months). During this period of college, the Navy pays for tuition, fees, and textbooks and provides uniforms and a subsistence allowance of $100 per month. At the beginning of the second year, students join the Marine Corps Reserve.

Four-Year College Program: Students are selected from those applying for enrollment at each Navy/Marine Corps unit. During the first year in the basic course, students have the status of civilians who have entered into a contract with the Navy. Upon enrollment in the advanced course, College Program students enlist in the Marine Corps Reserve. The Navy provides uniforms, Naval Science textbooks, and $100 a month subsistence allowance for a maximum of 20 months during the advanced course. Three-, two-, and one-year scholarships are available to College Program students applying to the Scholarship Program.

Two-Year College Program: Students who are selected are those with advanced college standing who qualify for enrollment in the advanced course. They must first successfully complete the six-week course at the Naval Science Institute. Those enrolled in the two-year College Program have the same privileges and obligations as those in the four-year College Program. The Navy provides uniforms, Naval Science textbooks, and $100 a month subsistence allowance for a maximum of 20 months during the advanced course.

Approximately 4.5 percent of scholarship and 11 percent of non-scholarship midshipmen are women, for a program total of about 6 percent.

Information about the College Program is available from any Navy/Marine Corps ROTC unit; these units are listed in the Appendix. For more detailed information about the Scholarship Program, contact a Marine Corps recruiting station, or write to Commandant of the Marine Corps, Code MRRO-6, Headquarters Marine Corps, Washington, DC 20380.

Mission

As was discussed earlier, the impetus for the modern Naval ROTC program came from the Holloway Plan, which was submitted to the Secretary of the Navy in 1945. That plan recommended that the requirements of Naval Science subjects in NROTC units, now called Shore Commands, be limited to those necessary to insure that the student attained an acceptable breadth of fundamental knowledge. At the same time, the midshipman was to be so trained that upon graduation he could perform his duties as an Ensign competently and effectively. These principles are still followed in the NROTC program.

Stated officially, the purpose of the Naval Reserve Officers Training Corps program is to educate, train, and retain select young men and women for careers as commissioned officers of the Regular Navy and Marine Corps. The young Ensigns and Second Lieutenants produced under the NROTC program supplement the graduates from the United States Naval Academy at Annapolis. Today, the NROTC Navy/Marine Corps Scholarship Program is the largest single source of Regular Navy and Marine Corps officers. As with the other service ROTC programs, completion of the ROTC program, even under scholarship, does not require the newly commissioned officer to commit to a 20- or 30-year career in the Navy or the Marine Corps. Most ROTC graduates serve on active duty for their obligated tours of three, four, or five years, enter the Reserve for three, four, or five years, and then return fully to civilian life. However, a significant percentage choose to make the Navy or Marine Corps a full-time career.

The mission of the US Navy is to conduct prompt and sustained combat operations at sea in support of national policy. The principal functions of the mission are sea control, power projection, and strategic sealift. These functions are closely related. A degree of sea control is mandatory in the area from which power is projected, and the ability of naval forces to project power was developed as a method of achieving or maintaining sea control. Additionally, the Navy's long-standing role of providing strategic sealift is now formally recognized as a third major function.

The Marine Corps is one of four separate military services within the Department of Defense. The Marine Corps and the Navy are separate services within the Department of the Navy. Title 10 of the US Code states in part that the Marine Corps shall:

- Provide Fleet Marine Forces of combined arms, together with supporting air components, for service with the fleet in the seizure or defense of advance naval bases and for the conduct of such land operations as may be essential to the prosecution of a naval campaign.
- Develop tactics, techniques, and equipment used by landing forces.
- Perform such other duties as the President may direct.

The Naval ROTC program then must carry out its mission of preparing young men and women for active duty based in part on the unique mission of the Navy and Marine Corps. The Naval ROTC unit fulfills its mission by providing a common curriculum for all midshipmen in the first two years of a four-year program, and then teaches Navy-specific subjects and Marine Corps-specific subjects in the last two years of the program.

Organization and Administration

Naval ROTC units are organized and administered in a slightly different fashion than are the Army and Air Force ROTC units. The Naval ROTC unit commander, either a Navy Captain or a Marine Corps Colonel, reports directly to the Chief of Naval Education and Training (CNET) at the Pensacola Naval Air Station in Pensacola, Florida. The CNET, usually a three-star Admiral, is responsible for all aspects of the Naval ROTC program on a nationwide basis. He reports directly to the Chief of Naval Personnel, Department of the Navy. The CNET is assisted in managing the NROTC by a Rear Admiral, who is responsible for overall Officer Professional Development as well as being the Deputy Chief, Naval Education and Training. The Rear Admiral is assisted by staff officers in the rank of Navy Captain who are charged with administering the NROTC and the junior NROTC programs. These staff officers deal directly with the NROTC Commanders and provide administrative support and guidance to the NROTC detachments, but they are not in the direct chain of command. The NROTC detachments are called Shore Commands, and the Professor of Naval Science is in a command position. He receives his command guidance directly from the Vice Admiral who fills the CNET position.

The Professor of Naval Science is the Commanding Officer of the NROTC unit. He is the head of the military unit and also a member of the faculty of the college or university. In addition to conducting the Naval Science syllabi and other Navy and Marine Corps functions, he and the officers on his staff counsel the midshipmen of the NROTC unit on personal matters and matters relating to their future in the Naval service. Depending upon the number of NROTC students at the particular institution, the midshipmen are usually organized into a battalion having three companies, which are composed of three platoons, each with three or more squads; each squad contains eight to ten men or women. The student chain of command is made up of midshipmen in their third and fourth year of the program. As the participants in the program receive more and more Naval training, they are put into positions of greater responsibility in the student chain of command. This system gives the students opportunities to develop and refine their leadership skills as well as obtain a better understanding of Naval operations. At most NROTC units this student chain of command is actively involved in running the NROTC program, with guidance and direction from the Professor of Naval Science and his staff.

If you enter into the NROTC program, it is definitely to your advantage to ask the advice and assistance of the NROTC staff on all unfamiliar matters, whether academic, military, or personal. They have a wealth of personal experience that can benefit you, and they want to help you get the most out of your college education and become a professional Navy or Marine Corp officer.

Naval Junior ROTC

The NJROTC program was established by Public Law 88-647 in 1964. The program is conducted at accredited senior high schools throughout the United States, including the District of Columbia and Guam. Instructors are retired Navy, Marine Corps, and Coast Guard officers and enlisted personnel. The classroom curriculum emphasizes citizenship, leadership, basic naval orientation, history, seamanship, navigation, engineering, and communications. Classroom academics are augmented throughout the year by rifle and drill teams, various school activities, orientation cruises, flights, visits to naval shore activities, and abbreviated recruit training. Uniforms, textbooks, training aids and devices, travel, a portion of instructors' salaries, and miscellaneous expenses are paid for by the Navy. Currently 233 high schools in the United States and Guam host the NJROTC program. No obligation is incurred by the young men and women who take NJROTC; however, young men and women who have taken NJROTC and then enter upon active duty have advantages over those who did not take NJROTC.

The goal of the NJROTC program is to develop responsible and informed citizens, a goal compatible with that of all secondary education in America today. The program is designed to encourage patriotism, discipline, and a high degree of personal honor. Additionally, emphasis is placed on technical and academic study of the development of the modern Navy. The program also promotes an appreciation of the fundamental concept of seapower and its importance in the US defense structure.

The NJROTC curriculum is adaptable to a three- or four-year program and encompasses 180 hours per academic year. The course

ship Program that is available to college students who complete their sophomore year or the third year in a five-year curriculum at an accredited college or university having a Navy ROTC program. When accepted, students attend the six-week Naval Science Institute at Newport, Rhode Island, during the summer between their sophomore and junior years to bring them up to date on the NROTC curriculum missed during their freshman and sophomore years. They are reimbursed for travel expenses to and from Newport and also receive pay during those six weeks. Procedures for applying for all scholarships can be obtained from NROTC units listed in the Appendix or from Navy and Marine Corps processing stations.

While the scholarship is in effect, the Navy pays tuition, costs of textbooks, fees of an instructional nature, and a subsistence allowance of $100 per month up to ten months per year. Midshipmen also receive training pay during summer training periods. The Navy provides uniforms, which are worn by the midshipmen during drills, summer training periods, and specified Naval Science classes.

Applicants for four-year scholarships should submit their application as early as possible after March 1 of the year they intend to enter college. Applications must be postmarked by December 1 to be considered for the next academic year. The applicant is responsible for making independent arrangements to take either the SAT or the ACT. The test scores must be released to the NROTC Scholarship Program and received by December 31 of the year preceding entry into the college or university. Applicants may authorize release of the test scores to the Program by marking the program code 0656 on the test registration form. SAT or ACT results are used to determine if the applicant is a finalist. The following College Board scores would probably ensure qualification as a finalist:

> Navy—SAT, verbal 430 and mathematics 520, English 18 and Mathematics 24
> Marine Corps—SAT, composite 1000; ACT, mathematics plus English, 45

NROTC candidates assume all responsibility for applying for admission to the NROTC college or colleges of their choice. Admission to an institution hosting an NROTC program must be received before the scholarship can be awarded. Applicants designated as NROTC finalists are required to indicate choice of colleges, in order of preference, when they complete the application form. The choice of college is not a factor in the selection process but is required for monitoring placement of those who are selected.

Preliminary screening is accomplished when the SAT or ACT test scores are reviewed together with other information on the applicant's questionnaire. Those who meet the qualifying standards are designated as finalists and requested to report to a Navy or Marine Corps processing station for an interview. Finalists are advised by letter where and when to report for an interview. The result of the interview is forwarded to Navy Recruiting Command headquarters with the complete application package.

Navy-Option Candidates: A selection board meets during November to conduct an early screening of Navy ROTC four-year scholarship candidates. All applications received at Navy Recruiting Command headquarters by late October are considered for early selection. Candidates selected are notified in December. Candidates not selected are automatically considered by the regular selection board, along with finalists whose applications were received after the early selection board deadline date. The second, or regular, meeting of the selection board is in February. Candidates selected are notified in March.

Since the early selection board can select only a limited number of candidates, failure to be selected early carries no negative or adverse reflection. The February selection board is completely unaware of which candidates were reviewed for early selection.

Each state, the District of Columbia, Puerto Rico, the Virgin Islands, Guam, and the Canal Zone is assigned a proportionate share of the Navy ROTC vacancies. Quotas are based on the percentage of finalists from each state or area. The competition in each state or territory is restricted to finalists who maintain legal residence in the state or territory.

Members of the two Navy selection boards are invited to serve in that capacity by the Commander, Navy Recruiting Command, and function under rules of complete impartiality. The various factors considered by the boards include not only high school records and College Board test scores, but also leadership potential, extracurricular activities, and aptitude for commissioned service. Information on physical qualifications is not a factor. The selection board designates principal and alternate selectees to receive scholarships for the next fall term. The selection process is competitive in nature. The best-qualified candidates are selected for the available quotas. Selections by the board are final.

Marine Corps-Option Candidates: The selection of Marine Corps-option candidates is made by boards convened at Headquarters, US Marine Corps, in November and February. The boards are composed of Marine Corps officers knowledgeable in the NROTC programs and contemporary educational requirements. Selection of candidates is made on a national basis. The boards consider educational achievement, demonstrated leadership, extracurricular activities, and aptitude for commissioned service.

The Chief of Naval Education and Training notifies the principal selectees as they are found physically qualified or a waiver is granted, and as acceptance by the NROTC college or university is confirmed. He also notifies alternate selectees if and when they are advanced to scholarship status. Notification may occur at any time from May 1 to September 1 (early selectees at any time after January 1 of the year college attendance begins). Sometime after July 1 selectees who were offered and accepted scholarships receive letters authorizing them to proceed at the prescribed time to designated colleges or universities. Reimbursement for travel expenses from home to school is made after appointment as a midshipman.

Upon commencement of the fall term, selectees are sworn in as midshipmen, Naval Reserve, and enrolled in the NROTC program. The subsistence allowance at the rate of $100 per month accrues from the date of acceptance of appointment.

Competition for all scholarships is keen. Students in college interested in applying for one of the awards should talk with the Navy and Marine representatives at the NROTC unit. Minor changes are made in all service scholarship programs annually as the needs of the services change. Students should work closely with the NROTC units.

Qualifications and Requirements

Eligibility requirements for the Scholarship Program and the College Program are similar, but those for the Scholarship Program are more stringent.

Applicants for the Scholarship Program must:

- Be a United States citizen.
- Be 17 years of age by September 1 of the year they accept the scholarship and enter the college or university, and less than 21 years of age on June 30 the year after accepting the scholarship. Those seeking a bachelor's degree requiring five years to complete must be less than 20 years old on June 30 of the year after accepting the scholarship. For all Scholarship Programs, applicants must not have reached their 25th birthday by June 30 of the calendar year in which graduation and commission-

ing are anticipated. Applicants who have prior active-duty military service may be eligible for age waivers for a time equal to their prior service on a month-for-month basis for a maximum of 48 months. Age waivers may be granted provided the 29th birthday will not be reached by June 30 of the calendar year in which graduation and commissioning are anticipated.

- Be a high school graduate or possess an equivalency certificate by the end of August of the calendar year prior to entrance into the four-year Scholarship Program. Two-year scholarship students must have completed at least one year of college-level calculus through differential and integral calculus of one real variable with a minimum grade of "C" and must be accepted for entrance into the NROTC college as a junior in a major acceptable to the Navy.
- Be physically qualified in accordance with Navy standards.
- Have no moral obligations or personal convictions that prevent conscientious bearing of arms and supporting and defending the Constitution of the United States against all enemies, foreign or domestic.
- Apply for and gain admission to the NROTC college or colleges of applicant's choice. Admission to an NROTC institution is not required during the selection process; however, admission must be received before the scholarship can be awarded.

If selected for a scholarship and upon enrollment in a NROTC Scholarship Program, students agree in writing to these requirements:

- To pursue academic majors of interest to the Navy or Marine Corps.
- To complete prescribed Naval Science courses, university courses, drills, and summer training periods.
- To accept a commission in the Regular Navy or Marine Corps, if offered.
- To serve a minimum of eight years in an active/inactive duty status from the date of acceptance of the commission. (The present program requires that at least four of the eight years be spent in an active-duty status.)
- To enlist in the United States Naval Reserve (USNR) for eight years in pay grade E-1 (seaman recruit) prior to being appointed midshipman, USNR, and receiving compensation.

Students disenrolling from an NROTC Scholarship Program for reasons beyond their control are discharged from their enlisted status. A minimum of two years of active enlisted service may be required of students who default from the terms of their NROTC contract after commencement of their sophomore year.

Scholarship students who default during their freshman year do not incur an active-duty commitment unless they were active-duty enlisted personnel released early for the purpose of accepting the scholarship. Those students have an enlisted service commitment equivalent to the time not served on their original enlistment contract when they were discharged or separated to accept an NROTC scholarship.

Applicants for the College Program must:

- Be a United States citizen.
- Be at least 17 years of age and not have reached 27½ by June 30 of the year of college graduation. (Students may enroll in the College Program at 16 if the NROTC unit Commanding Officer considers them mature enough to take Naval Science courses.)
- Be a high school graduate or possess an equivalent certificate by the end of August of the calendar year prior to entrance into the program.
- Be physically qualified in accordance with Navy standards.
- Have a satisfactory record of moral integrity, academic and extracurricular activities, and potential officer characteristics.
- Have no moral obligations or personal convictions that prevent conscientious bearing of arms and supporting and defending the Constitution of the United States against all enemies, foreign or domestic.
- Have been accepted for admission as a civilian student to an NROTC college or university. Students attending an accredited college or university in the vicinity of an NROTC institution may enroll in the NROTC institution's College Program if such a crosstown enrollment has been approved by officials of both schools, the Professor of Naval Science, and the Chief of Naval Education and Training. (The list of colleges with NROTC programs, including those accepting crosstown enrollment, is given in the Appendix.)

All applicants for the NROTC program must be accepted by the Professor of Naval Science; acceptance into the program is not automatic.

General Physical Requirements. Generally speaking, physical requirements to gain admission to the Naval ROTC program are more stringent than those for the Army and Air Force ROTC programs. Following are some of the significant requirements.

HEIGHT   Men: Navy, 62 to 78 inches.
              Marines, 66 to 78 inches.

          Women: Navy, 60 to 78 inches.
                 Marines, 60 to 78 inches.

WEIGHT   Proportionate to height.

EYES   20/20 each eye without correction. Limited waivers available for those whose vision corrects to 20/20 in both eyes where refractive error in each eye does not exceed ±5.50 diopters. Both eyes must be free of any disfiguring or incapacitating abnormality and from acute or chronic disease. Normal color vision is required for Navy ROTC candidates. Marine Corps-option candidates have no color vision requirements.

ALLERGIES   No severe hay fever or chronic rhinitis. No history of asthma since 12th birthday.

HEART   Normal heartbeat. No hypertension or history of cardiovascular ailment.

JOINTS   No internal derangement or residuals of serious injury.

TEETH   Excellent dental health. Minimum of eight serviceable teeth each arch.

The Department of Defense Medical Examination Review Board schedules and reviews physical examinations of candidates for the four-year Scholarship Program, other ROTC scholarship programs, and the service academies. Candidates applying for more than one military program normally receive only one physical examination. Those who have correctable physical defects should have them taken care of before reporting for the medical examination.

Physical status is determined independently of the scholarship selection process. The selection committee is not aware of the physical status of any candidate at the time of their meeting, and no candidate's record is withheld from selection board consideration because of less than full physical qualification.

Scholarship selections are limited in number, and competition is keen. Therefore, candidates should use their best judgment with regard to undergoing any extensive corrective procedure recommended by the Medical Examination Review Board as long as their selection status remains unknown. Women who are pregnant at the time of entry into college are ineligible to participate in the NROTC program.

In the qualifications and requirements for the Naval ROTC program, it is advisable to check with the NROTC unit on the college campus for possible changes.

Special Programs

Both the Navy and the Marine Corps offer special programs of education and training that benefit both the individual and the service. These programs are available to NROTC graduates as well as college seniors in special fields who have not taken NROTC while in college. The requirements, eligibility criteria, and obligations incurred from participation in these programs change frequently; it is advisable to check with the NROTC unit or with Navy/Marine Corps processing stations to determine the latest requirements.

Naval pilot training is available to qualified commissioned officers of the Aviation Officer Candidate School, the US Naval Academy, or NROTC. Primary flight training begins at either Milton, Florida, or Corpus Christi, Texas. Upon completion of primary flight training, students receive orders for one of three aviation pipelines: jet, prop, or helicopter. After successful completion of advanced flight training, students receive their wings and are designated Naval Aviators. Active-duty obligation is five years from the date of designation as a Naval Aviator. The total time in training is approximately 18 months.

Naval Flight Officer Training is available to qualified commissioned officers of the Aviation Officer Candidate School, the US Naval Academy, or NROTC. After the completion of basic navigation training, officers have the opportunity to specialize and receive advanced training in one of the following categories: airborne early warning systems operator, air antisubmarine warfare tactical coordinator, or airborne electronics countermeasure systems operator. The active-duty obligation is five years from the date of designation as a Naval Flight Officer.

Navy Aeronautical Engineering Duty Officer/Aviation Maintenance is a program for those who wish to become specialists in the aviation maintenance field. Applicants for this program should be seniors in college or graduates in a technical management major, although those with other majors may be considered eligible. Selected candidates receive orders to Aviation Officer Candidate School at Pensacola, Florida. Upon successful completion of 14 weeks of familiarization training, a candidate is commissioned as an Ensign in the Naval Reserve and undergoes about 16 weeks of instruction at the Naval Air Training Center, Millington, Tennessee. Age limits are 19 to 35 at the time of commissioning; service obligation is four years from the date of commissioning.

Naval Aviation Officer Candidate School is open to qualified graduates of regionally accredited colleges. The candidates receive 14 weeks of rigorous academic, military, and physical training at Pensacola, Florida. Successful candidates are commissioned as Ensigns in the Naval Reserve and serve on active duty as either unrestricted or restricted line officers. Age limits at commissioning are 19 to 29 for Naval Aviators and Naval Flight Officers; 19 to 35

The marching band at Georgia Tech.

for aviation maintenance duty officers and special duty intelligence officers. The obligated service is four years from the date of commissioning.

Naval Aviation Officer Candidate–Special Duty Intelligence is a program for training as an Intelligence Special Duty Officer in a nonflying assignment. Applications may be made during the senior year of college or after graduation. After 14 weeks of training, candidates are commissioned Ensigns in the Naval Reserve and report to the Armed Forces Intelligence Institute at Lowry Air Force Base, Denver, Colorado, for approximately 20 weeks of training. Candidates serve on active duty for four years from the time of commissioning. Age limits are 19 to 35 at the time of commissioning.

The Navy, like the Army and Air Force, offers attractive programs of financial assistance to students in certain medical programs in return for specified periods of military service. Medical students who qualify receive tuition, books, fees, and a monthly stipend. The obligated service is a minimum of three years.

The Navy offers a wide range of educational opportunities for both officers and enlisted personnel. Naval personnel are able to pursue all levels of education and training no matter where they are stationed. An outstanding program is the opportunity to study at the Naval Postgraduate School at Monterey, California. Naval officers are eligible to attend this institution, which is noted for its outstanding faculty of scientists and educators. After four years of active-duty commissioned service, qualified Navy officers may be invited to Monterey to study advanced engineering and technical and managerial disciplines that are particularly relevant to the Navy. They may also earn advanced degrees in programs accepted by leading accrediting and professional associations. While attending the Naval Postgraduate School, officers continue to receive full Navy pay, benefits, and allowances.

The Marine Corps also offers several commissioning programs other than the standard NROTC program. Under the Officer Candidate programs, male and female graduates of an accredited four-year college or university are eligible for Reserve commissions as ground officers. In addition, male officers are eligible for commissioning as aviators. Upon successful completion of a 10-week screening and training program, candidates are commissioned as Second Lieutenants in the Marine Corps Reserve. Upon completion of this program and precommissioning training, candidates are assigned to the Basic School at Quantico, Virginia, for 23 weeks of officer training. Aviation officers receive additional training for 12 to 18 months. Ground officers have an active-duty obligation of three years after commissioning; aviators (pilots and flight officers) have an active-duty obligation of four and one half years after designation as a pilot or flight officer. Aviation candidates must be at least 20 years old upon entering the program and no older than 27½ years upon commissioning. Ground officers must be no older than 28 upon commissioning.

Marine Platoon Leaders Class (PLC) is available to full-time physically qualified male undergraduate freshmen, sophomores, and juniors attending accredited colleges. Precommissioning training consists of two six-week sessions or one ten-week training session during summer vacation(s) at the Marine Corps Development and Education Command, Quantico. PLC students may choose ground, aviation, or law training and may apply for financial assistance of $100 per month upon completion of at least one summer training session. Aviation students may join the Flight Indoctrination Program and receive civilian flight instruction during their senior year of college. Upon graduation from college, PLC participants receive commissions as Second Lieutenants in the Marine Corps Reserve. Officers are assigned to the Basic School at Quantico for 23 weeks of basic officer training. Students opting for ground or law training must be at least 17 years old upon entering the program and no older than 28 upon commissioning. Pilot candidates must be at least 17 upon entering the program and no older than 27½ upon commissioning. Minimum active-duty obligation for ground officers and lawyers following commissioning is three years. Following flight training and designation as a Naval Aviator, minimum active-duty obligation is four and one half years. Depending on the amount of financial assistance received, minimum active-duty requirements may be extended.

All male Marine Corps commissioned officers between the ages of 20 and 27½ are eligible to apply for pilot or naval flight officer training. Pilot training begins with 12 to 18 months at the Naval Air Training Command, Pensacola, Florida, followed by an assignment to one of the many Marine Corps aircraft squadrons (jet fighter, jet attack, helicopter, or multiengine transport). Flight officers are also trained at the Naval Air Training Command in Pensacola, studying for approximately eight months before assignment to one of the Marine Corps aircraft squadrons. Either assignment requires a four-and-one-half-year commitment after designation as an aviator.

Marines, regardless of rank or duty station, are encouraged to further their education. The Marine Corps has many programs that provide tuition assistance and other financial aid to be used in pursuit of advanced degrees. Programs are available that allow Marine officers to attend college full time while receiving full pay and allowances. If you are interested in learning details on programs such as the Advanced Degree Program, the Funded Legal Education Program, or the Special Education Program, contact the NROTC representatives. The opportunity to continue your education at government expense is one of the most attractive features of a military career.

Curriculum

The military commander of an NROTC unit is either a Commander or Captain in the Navy or a Colonel in the Marine Corps, and as the Professor of Naval Science of the NROTC unit is also a member of the college faculty. In addition to administering the Naval Science curriculum and conducting other Naval functions, the Professor of Naval Science and the officers on his or her staff serve as counselors to midshipmen on personal and academic matters. All NROTC units have both Navy and Marine Corps officers to insure that they can provide informed counsel to both the Navy-option and Marine Corps-option midshipmen.

Scholarship Program students and College Program students take the same Naval Science courses; the Scholarship Program students are required to take certain additional academic and elective courses. Marine Corps-option students take Marine Corps–oriented Naval Science courses in their junior and senior years. Scholarship and College Program NROTC students are required to complete the NROTC academic and professional program, which consists of four parts: the academic major, which must be in a field of study of interest to the Navy or Marine Corps; Navy-specified college courses; Naval professional academic courses (Naval Science courses), and Naval professional training.

Students in the Navy-option Scholarship Program are strongly encouraged to pursue majors in engineering and approved sciences to meet the technological requirements of the Navy. Fields of study must have direct applicability to the Navy mission, such as chemistry, computer science, mathematics, oceanography, operations analysis, physical science, physics, and all types of engineering. Navy-option College Program students do not have as many restrictions on their academic major, but they are still encouraged to pursue degrees in engineering, mathematics, and science. Some Navy-option College Program students pursue degrees in other fields such as international relations, journalism, and the humanities, but these students are not as competitive in the Navy as are their counterparts who major in technical and engineering fields. Marine Corps-option Scholarship and College Program students have no restrictions on academic majors, but the Professor of Naval Science, with the assistance of the Marine Corps officer instructor, screens proposed academic majors and guides the students to select areas considered beneficial to the Marine Corps and to the individual concerned for a career as a Marine Corps officer.

Navy-Specified College Courses

The following courses, taught by civilian faculty, are required/recommended for all NROTC students:

Title	Year Normally Taken	Required/Recommended
Calculus (differential and integral)	freshman/sophomore	Required of all Navy-option scholarship students. Recommended for all others.
General physics (calculus-based)	sophomore/junior	Required of all Navy-option scholarship students. Recommended for all others.
College algebra or higher level	freshman-junior	Required of all Navy-option College Program students.
Physical science	sophomore-senior	Required of all Navy-option College Program students.
Modern Indo-European or Asiatic language	freshman-senior	Required of all NROTC scholarship students. Recommended for College Program students.
Technical electives	freshman/senior	Required of all Navy-option scholarship students not majoring in a technical curriculum.
Marine-option electives	junior/senior	Required of all Marine-option students.
American Military History		Recommended for all NROTC students.
National Security Policy		Recommended for all NROTC students.

Naval Professional Academic Courses (Naval Science courses)

Title	Year Taken	Required of
Introduction to Naval Science	freshman	all
Naval Ships Systems I (engineering)	freshman	all
Naval Ships Systems II (weapons)	sophomore	all
Seapower and Maritime Affairs	sophomore	all
Navigation and Naval Operations I	junior	Navy-option
Navigation and Naval Operations II	junior	Navy-option
Evolution of Warfare	junior	Marine-option
Leadership and Management I	senior	Navy-option
Leadership and Management II	senior	Navy-option
Amphibious Warfare	senior	Marine-option
Naval Laboratory	all	all
Naval Science Institute	sophomore summer	all two-year program entrants

The curriculum is varied and stimulating. The primary purpose of all the instruction is to prepare and educate the young men and women for commissioning in the unrestricted line in the Navy and Marine Corps. Active-duty Navy and Marine Corps officers present the instruction, and they are able to provide realism and applicability based on their own experience. Students who have not had prior NROTC instruction and who want to enter the NROTC program in their junior year must attend the Naval Science Institute in the summer after completing their sophomore year. The Institute offers an intensive six-week professional, academic, and training program designed to prepare the student for entry into the program. The course covers the academic subjects taught in the first two years of the NROTC program and is the equivalent of the NROTC basic course.

Navy Professional Training

Professional training is an important part of the NROTC program, and it is conducted both on and off campus. The Naval laboratory is a weekly laboratory, normally two hours in length, conducted during each academic term. Emphasis is on professional training of a nonacademic nature. The laboratory is intended for topics such as drill and ceremonies, physical fitness and swimming testing, cruise preparation, cruise evaluation, sail training, safety awareness, preparation for commissioning, personal finances, insurance, and applied exercises in Naval ship systems, navigation,

Naval operations, Naval administration, and military justice. Other special topics and briefings are conducted as required. Professors of Naval Science also conduct new-student orientations, assisted by their staff and the midshipmen staff. The orientations are designed to insure a smooth transition for the NROTC students coming in from high schools and also to help publicize the NROTC program.

Summer Training

Summer training periods are held annually to enable NROTC students to gain experience in the practical application of their studies in Naval science. These programs, normally four to eight weeks in length, are three in number:

Third Class summer training, conducted between the freshman and sophomore academic years for scholarship students. It is normally at-sea training.

Second Class summer training, conducted between the sophomore and junior academic years for scholarship students. It is normally career orientation and training for midshipmen. The training is conducted at various Naval installations, and students are provided orientation in aviation, submarines, surface warfare, and amphibious operations.

First Class summer training, conducted between the junior and senior academic years for all NROTC students. It is normally at-sea training for Navy-option midshipmen, and "Bulldog training" at the Marine Corps Development and Education Command, Quantico, Virginia, for Marine-option midshipmen. For Navy-option personnel, the training aboard various elements of the fleet provides orientation to the duties of enlisted and junior officer personnel. The "Bulldog training" provides the Marine-option personnel basic preparation for commissioning as Marine Second Lieutenants. College Program students attend one summer training period only, between the junior and senior academic years.

The Navy also supervises another program during the summer months. To promote an exchange of professional, cultural, and social experiences between midshipmen in the US Navy and midshipmen of some 25 foreign navies, a Foreign Exchange Midshipmen Training Program normally is operated each summer. A limited number of exemplary career-motivated First Class midshipmen who are proficient in the language involved are ordered to training in a ship of one of the foreign navies in lieu of the normal First Class training period. Similarly, a small number of midshipmen of those navies undergo at-sea training in ships of the US Navy.

Indoctrination Field Trips and Visits

The professional development of NROTC students extends beyond the study of Naval Science on campus and summer training. Off-campus field trips are important aspects of training that take on a variety of forms as allowed by available opportunities. Visits to Navy and Marine Corps bases, surface ship and nuclear submarine field trips, and aviation indoctrination visits are typical events that help motivate students and prepare them for future Navy service. Additional periods of training for practice cruises and special requirements may also become available to NROTC students during the four-year training program. NROTC students are paid for the summer training periods and are reimbursed for travel to the training sites. The training programs are designed to assist the newly commissioned officer in making a smooth transition from college life to active duty in the Navy or Marine Corps. Midshipmen, both men and women, who feel confident in their technical knowledge and who have had actual hands-on experience onboard ship or at military installations have the best chance of being successful in their new careers.

ROTC Campus Activities

NROTC midshipmen lead essentially the same campus life as other undergraduates. They make their own arrangements for enrollment and room and board; pursue academic studies leading to a bachelor's degree; and may participate in any extracurricular activities that do not interfere with their NROTC requirements. Moreover, the midshipmen have an advantage over the non-NROTC students in that they are offered the services of additional advisors and counselors on the NROTC staff. These active-duty officers assist the midshipmen with personal and academic matters. In many cases, these officers can assist greatly in helping the NROTC student adjust more easily to the college or university experience.

NROTC students taking science and engineering courses have relatively little free time, particularly if they must find employment to defray part of their living expenses. Even when ROTC students have received a full four-year scholarship, many of them choose to find part-time work to meet their expenses. These midshipmen still find time to participate in campus NROTC activities such as drill-teams, rifle and pistol teams, fund-raising marathon runs, and civic projects. NROTC students are eligible to participate in the national military society, the Pershing Rifles, which was described earlier.

NROTC students must conform to the high standards of academic performance, honorable conduct, and gentlemanly courtesy required by both the US Navy and the institution in which they are enrolled. In addition, they must conduct themselves in a military manner at all times while under Naval jurisdiction, while attending Naval Science classes, drills and exercises, off-campus visits to Navy or Marine bases, and during the summer training periods.

The Navy expects that the graduates of NROTC colleges and universities will be of a caliber comparable to those of the Naval Academy, and that all will be bound together in a common purpose by the ties of brotherhood traditional in the Naval service. The Navy expects its officers, both Navy and Marine Corps, to adhere to the ideals expressed by John Paul Jones in a statement to the Maritime Commission in 1775:

"It is by no means enough that an Officer of the Navy should be a capable mariner. He must be that, of course, but also a great deal more. He should be, as well, a gentleman of liberal education, refined manner, punctilious courtesy, and the nicest sense of personal honor.

"He should be the soul of tact, patience, justice, firmness, and charity. No meritorious act of a subordinate should escape his attention or be left to pass without its reward, even if the reward be only a word of approval. Conversely, he should not be blind to a single fault in any subordinate, though, at the same time, he should be quick and unfailing to distinguish error from malice, thoughtlessness from incompetency, and well-meant shortcoming from heedless and stupid blunder. As he should be universal and impartial in his rewards and approval of merit, so should he be judicial and unbending in his punishment or reproof of misconduct."

Assignments and Obligations

Upon satisfactory completion of Naval Science and bachelor's degree requirements, a midshipman transfers from reserve status to active duty and receives a commission as a Regular Officer in the

Naval service. NROTC graduates have an equal opportunity with their contemporaries for promotion and eventual progression to the rank of Admiral in the Navy or General in the Marine Corps. Promotion is earned by continued growth through professional study and demonstrated competence in assigned duties. Few professions hold greater promise for the ambitious man or woman than a career in the Navy or Marine Corps.

Navy ROTC Graduates

A newly commissioned male Ensign is normally assigned to duty aboard a surface ship, a nuclear-powered submarine, or an aviation squadron, after a period of specialized training in the appropriate warfare specialty. Women officers are usually assigned to duty at shore activities; however, a limited number of women may be assigned to noncombatant ships and to aviation squadrons.

The new Ensign assigned aboard a surface ship undergoes approximately four months of specialized surface warfare training and an additional year of graduate-level schooling if approved for nuclear propulsion training. Successful completion of this instruction leads to duty on a variety of classes of surface ships including aircraft carriers, cruisers, frigates, destroyers, amphibious ships, and auxiliary ships.

The prospective submariner enters a program of one year of graduate-level schooling in nuclear propulsion and nine weeks of submarine training. Successful completion of this program leads to duty aboard ballistic missile and attack submarines.

The prospective aviation officer enters a program of approximately one year of pilot or naval flight officer instruction. Successful completion of this training leads to designation as a Naval Aviator or Naval Flight Officer.

Marine Corps-Option Graduates

Marine Corps midshipmen participate in the same basic program as Navy ROTC midshipmen for the first two years, including a summer session of military training. Beginning with the junior year, Marine Corps midshipmen are taught Marine Corps-oriented courses and are counseled on the duties and opportunities awaiting them as Marine Corps officers.

All newly commissioned Marine Corps Second Lieutenants are assigned to the Basic School at Quantico, Virginia, where intensive

Marine training begins. After the Basic School, which lasts six months, several occupational fields are available for further training and assignment. These include Marine infantry, aviation, artillery, tracked vehicles, engineering, communications, supply administration, and computer science, among others.

Marine Corps officers selected for aviation receive flight training at Naval Air Station, Pensacola, Florida, where they can learn to fly helicopters, multiengine, or high-performance jet aircraft. Following the Basic School and advanced training in the assigned occupational field, most Marine Lieutenants are assigned to the Fleet Marine Force of the Marine Corps. This duty could be anywhere in the world.

All men and women who successfully complete the NROTC program and receive a commission as an Ensign in the Navy or as a Second Lieutenant in the Marine Corps are obligated to serve a total of eight years with the respective service. However, this eight years is divided differently between active duty and inactive duty depending on several factors. All newly commissioned officers who were graduated from the Scholarship Program must serve at least four years on active duty and the remaining time in the inactive Reserve. College Program students serve three years on active duty and five years in the Reserve. If the newly commissioned officers enter specialized training such as aviation or the nuclear program, they incur an additional year of active duty after the specialized training is completed. Thus, after the new Ensign had finished 13 months of aviation training, he would have a five-year active duty obligation. In the matter of obligations, just as in other aspects of the ROTC program, the prospective ROTC student is well advised to discuss in detail what is required of him or her with the ROTC staff on campus.

Conclusion

The culmination of all the hard work that goes into successfully completing the rigorous ROTC programs is the awarding of a commission as a Second Lieutenant or Ensign in our nation's armed forces. The commissioning ceremony is both a solemn and a joyous occasion. It is a proud moment in the life of dedicated young men and women, and it is usually attended by their friends and parents. All the newly commissioned officers take an oath of office in which they pledge their faithful service to the United States of America:

The Oath of Office

I, (first name, middle name, last name, and service number), having been appointed an officer in the Army (Navy, Air Force, Marine Corps) of the United States, in the grade of Second Lieutenant (Ensign), do solemnly swear (or affirm) that I will support and defend the Constitution of the United States against all enemies, foreign and domestic; that I take this obligation freely, without any mental reservation or purpose of evasion; and that I will well and faithfully discharge the duties of the office upon which I am about to enter, so help me God.

This oath must be understood by all the officers: It is a personal statement, made freely without qualification, that the officer will conscientiously and faithfully serve the United States of America.

Today, the armed forces have a tremendous need for well-educated men and women from all disciplines—military, scientific, technical, and humanistic. The economic, scientific, political, cultural, and social implications of high-level military decisions that are made almost daily must be studied and evaluated by the most knowledgeable minds in the United States. Those decisions are made by men and women wearing the uniforms of the armed forces. This analytical and creative thinking is responsive to the education, training, experience, and self-discipline acquired through years of dedicated service.

That is the challenge facing young men and women of this country today—the opportunity to serve the nation as professional officers in the armed forces. The challenge can only become more difficult in the years ahead as the United States and the rest of the world must deal with increasingly difficult problems of resource shortages, overpopulation, nuclear arms races, space exploration, and complicated international relations. Qualified ROTC graduates from our colleges and universities go on active duty as well-trained junior officers who have the opportunity to affect the future. These young men and women are an important part of the future.

This book has been written to give the prospective ROTC candidate and his or her parents, guidance counselors, ROTC instructors, and the public at large an appreciation of the ROTC program. ROTC provides valuable training for the individual and a great service for the nation. The ROTC programs are designed to attract, select, train, and retain the most outstanding high school graduates for regular and reserve careers in the armed forces.

The many benefits, both financial and otherwise, that accrue to the ROTC student during his or her college days have already been described. The book would be incomplete, however, without mentioning some of the many benefits for officers on active duty in the services. All officers follow a career pattern that offers constantly increasing responsibilities. Indeed, one of the major appeals of a service career is the fact that the young Second Lieutenant is given responsibility immediately upon entering the armed forces. All officers are assured of consideration for promotion at stated periods of service, and the competent and capable officer is reasonably assured of being promoted to the rank of Lieutenant Colonel in the Army, Air Force, or Marine Corps or to Commander in the Navy. Promotion is earned by continued growth through professional study and dedication and performance demonstrated by results.

In addition to regular pay and subsistence and quarters allowances, officers receive medical care for themselves and their dependents, as well as base exchange and commissary privileges. All services encourage officers to continue personal growth and education and in many cases provide funding for formal postgraduate education in various disciplines and specialties. These opportunities become available throughout the officer's career. Officers also receive a 30-day leave with pay each year. The Soldiers' and Sailors'

Civil Relief Act was designed primarily to insure that service personnel would not be penalized unfairly by tax liabilities, and in some cases service personnel receive tax advantages because of their service status. Service families enjoy a close-knit and varied social life with other service families, and also have opportunities to travel and live in different communities both in the United States and in foreign countries. The children of service members experience many varied situations and seem to benefit from being exposed to different customs and cultures. The current retirement system for military officers is very attractive, with the opportunity to retire at an early age with excellent retirement income.

While I served as a Professor of Military Science, I had the opportunity to talk seriously with many young men and women as to what they wanted most out of a service career or even a short tour on active duty. Most of them expressed the idea that they wanted "job satisfaction." They wanted to feel that what they did in the service "mattered" and that they would have both a decision about things that occurred and an effect on what occurred at their jobs. They did not want to become an unthinking, unfeeling part of a great impersonal bureaucratic machine.

To be productive and effective, every man and woman needs to

Formal dress whites inspection.

feel job satisfaction in his or her chosen career field. A "job" in this sense does not mean being paid for working at a task from nine to five and then rushing home to forget about it. Men and women in the armed forces serving as officers feel real satisfaction and fulfillment in accomplishing their work. A service career is an occupation and a profession in which the officer has total involvement. It is also a demanding career that calls for sacrifice, family separation at times, and a desire to serve your country.

Fortunately, many young men and women in the United States have high ideals and a deep sense of patriotism. In talking with my students and with many students in other service ROTC programs, I was greatly impressed with the seriousness of purpose and sense of real values of many college men and women. They expressed a desire to contribute to the security of the United States and to render important service to our society. It isn't a high-salaried job and material advantages that they are seeking; rather, it is the opportunity to serve a useful purpose in the world. Their high aspirations are compelling and the career that they finally settle on must satisfy both their intellectual and emotional requirements and the vital human need of fulfillment of life through work that is worthy of a person's full effort.

For many of these young men and women, the answer may well be found in a career in the armed forces. It is a life of service and dedication to country and one of traditional honor and prestige. Few fields hold greater promise for an ambitious young person seeking immediate responsibility, and no other field so combines adventure and security. There are opportunities for education and growth, travel and inspiring experiences. Officers know that their duties are vital to the security of the nation, and they welcome the growing responsibilities for the common welfare that come as they mature. It is a demanding life of challenge and change, unlimited opportunities, and high goals, and it brings rich rewards to the men and women who dedicate themselves and all their abilities to it. Our world is not so much inherited from our ancestors as it is on loan from our children. Our armed forces insure that we are able to pass on that world to our children.

Appendix

If you wish more specific information about individual service ROTC programs, you may write to the addresses listed below. These offices will be glad to respond to your specific questions about all aspects of the ROTC programs.

ARMY   Headquarters
         US Army Training and Doctrine Command
         (ROTC)
         Fort Monroe, VA 23651

AIR FORCE Headquarters
         DCS Technical Training (ROTC)
         Air Training Command
         Randolph Air Force Base, TX 78150

NAVY   Headquarters
         Naval Education and Training (ROTC)
         Naval Air Station
         Pensacola, FL 32508

ARMY ROTC COLLEGES AND UNIVERSITIES

ALABAMA
 Alabama A&M University, Normal
 Auburn Univ., Auburn
***Auburn Univ. at Montgomery, Montgomery
 Jacksonville State Univ., Jacksonville
**Marion Military Institute, Marion
 Tuskegee Institute, Tuskegee
 Univ. of Alabama, University
 Univ. of Alabama, Birmingham, Birmingham
 Univ. of North Alabama, Florence
 Univ. of South Alabama, Mobile

ALASKA
 Univ. of Alaska-Fairbanks, Fairbanks

Monthly Basic Pay Effective Oct. 1, 1985

GRADE	Under 2	2	3	4	6	8	10	12	14	16	18	20	22	26
COMMISSIONED OFFICERS														
O-10	5221.50	5405.40	5405.40	5405.40	5405.40	5612.70	5612.70	5724.90	5724.90	5724.90	5724.90	5724.90	5724.90	5724.90
O-9	4627.80	4749.00	4850.10	4850.10	4850.10	4973.40	4973.40	5180.40	5180.40	5612.70	5612.70	5724.90	5724.90	5724.90
O-8	4191.60	4317.00	4419.60	4419.60	4419.60	4749.00	4749.00	4973.40	4973.40	5180.40	5405.40	5612.70	5724.90	5724.90
O-7	3483.00	3719.70	3719.70	3719.70	3886.20	3886.20	4111.80	4111.80	4317.00	4749.00	5075.40	5075.40	5075.40	5075.40
O-6	2581.50	2836.20	3021.90	3021.90	3021.90	3021.90	3021.90	3021.90	3124.50	3618.60	3803.70	3886.20	4111.80	4459.50
O-5	2064.60	2424.60	2592.00	2592.00	2592.00	2592.00	2670.60	2814.00	3002.70	3227.10	3412.50	3515.70	3638.40	3638.40
O-4	1740.30	2119.20	2260.50	2260.50	2302.50	2404.20	2568.00	2712.60	2836.20	2960.70	3042.60	3042.60	3042.60	3042.60
O-3	1617.30	1808.10	1932.90	2138.70	2241.00	2321.70	2447.10	2568.00	2631.30	2631.30	2631.30	2631.30	2631.30	2631.30
O-2	1410.30	1540.20	1850.10	1912.50	1952.70	1952.70	1952.70	1952.70	1952.70	1952.70	1952.70	1952.70	1952.70	1952.70
O-1	1224.30	1274.70	1540.20	1540.20	1540.20	1540.20	1540.20	1540.20	1540.20	1540.20	1540.20	1540.20	1540.20	1540.20
COMMISSIONED OFFICERS WITH MORE THAN 4 YEARS ACTIVE DUTY AS ENLISTED OR WARRANT OFFICER														
O-3E	0.00	0.00	0.00	2138.70	2241.00	2321.70	2447.10	2568.00	2568.00	2670.60	2670.60	2670.60	2670.60	2670.70
O-2E	0.00	0.00	0.00	1912.50	1952.70	2014.50	2119.20	2200.20	2260.20	2260.50	2260.50	2260.50	2260.50	2260.50
O-1E	0.00	0.00	0.00	1540.20	1645.20	1705.80	1767.60	1829.10	1912.50	1912.50	1912.50	1912.50	1912.50	1912.50
WARRANT OFFICERS														
W-4	1647.60	1767.60	1767.60	1808.10	1890.30	1973.70	2056.50	2200.20	2302.50	2383.20	2447.10	2526.00	2610.60	2814.00
W-3	1497.30	1624.50	1624.50	1645.20	1664.70	1786.20	1890.30	1952.70	2014.50	2074.50	2138.70	2221.80	2302.50	2383.20
W-2	1311.60	1419.00	1419.00	1460.40	1540.20	1624.50	1686.00	1747.80	1808.10	1871.40	1932.90	1994.10	2074.50	2074.50
W-1	1092.90	1253.10	1253.10	1357.50	1419.00	1479.90	1540.20	1604.10	1664.70	1726.20	1786.20	1850.10	1850.10	1850.10
ENLISTED MEMBERS														
E-9	0.00	0.00	0.00	0.00	0.00	0.00	1916.40	1959.90	2004.30	2050.20	2095.80	2136.60	2249.10	2467.80
E-8	0.00	0.00	0.00	0.00	0.00	1607.40	1653.00	1696.50	1740.90	1786.50	1827.90	1872.90	1983.00	2204.10
E-7	1122.30	1211.40	1256.40	1300.20	1344.90	1387.50	1431.90	1476.30	1543.20	1587.00	1631.40	1652.70	1763.70	1983.00
E-6	965.40	1052.40	1096.20	1143.00	1185.30	1228.50	1273.80	1339.20	1381.20	1425.60	1447.50	1447.50	1447.50	1447.50
E-5	847.20	922.50	966.90	1009.20	1075.20	1119.00	1163.70	1206.30	1228.50	1228.50	1228.50	1228.50	1228.50	1228.50
E-4	790.50	834.60	883.50	952.20	989.70	989.70	989.70	989.70	989.70	989.70	989.70	989.70	989.70	989.70
E-3	744.60	785.10	816.90	849.30	849.30	849.30	849.30	849.30	849.30	849.30	849.30	849.30	849.30	849.30
E-2	716.40	716.40	716.40	716.40	716.40	716.40	716.40	716.40	716.40	716.40	716.40	716.40	716.40	716.40
E-1	639.00	639.00	639.00	639.00	639.00	639.00	639.00	639.00	639.00	639.00	639.00	639.00	639.00	639.00

ARIZONA
Arizona State Univ., Tempe
Northern Arizona Univ., Flagstaff
Univ. of Arizona, Tucson

ARKANSAS
Arkansas State Univ., State University
Arkansas Tech Univ., Russellville
Henderson State Univ., Arkadelphia
Ouachita Baptist Univ., Arkadelphia
Southern Arkansas Univ., Magnolia
Univ. of Arkansas, Fayetteville
Univ. of Arkansas, Little Rock, Little Rock
***Univ. of Arkansas at Monticello, Monticello
Univ. of Arkansas at Pine Bluff, Pine Bluff
Univ. of Central Arkansas, Conway

CALIFORNIA
California Polytechnic State Univ., San Luis Obispo
***California State College-San Bernardino, San Bernardino
***California State Polytechnic Univ.-Pomona, Pomona
California State Univ. at Fresno, Fresno
***California State Univ. at Long Beach, Long Beach
***California State Univ.-Fullerton, Fullerton
San Diego State Univ., San Diego
San Jose State Univ., San Jose
The Claremont Colleges, Claremont
Univ. of California-Berkeley, Berkeley
Univ. of California-Davis, Davis
Univ. of California-Los Angeles, Los Angeles
Univ. of California-Santa Barbara, Santa Barbara
Univ. of San Francisco, San Francisco
Univ. of Santa Clara, Santa Clara
Univ. of Southern California, Los Angeles

COLORADO
Colorado School of Mines, Golden
Colorado State Univ., Fort Collins
***Mesa College, Grand Junction
Metropolitan State College, Denver
Univ. of Colorado, Boulder
Univ. of Colorado at Colorado Springs, Colorado Springs
Univ. of Southern Colorado, Pueblo

CONNECTICUT
***Greater Hartford Campus, Univ. of Connecticut, Hartford
Univ. of Connecticut, Storrs
***Univ. of Bridgeport, Bridgeport

DELAWARE
Univ. of Delaware, Newark

DISTRICT OF COLUMBIA
Georgetown Univ., Washington
Howard Univ., Washington

FLORIDA
Embry-Riddle Aeronautical Univ., Daytona Beach
Florida A&M Univ., Tallahassee
Florida Institute of Technology, Melbourne
Florida Southern College, Lakeland
Florida State Univ., Tallahassee
***Saint Leo College, Saint Leo
Stetson Univ., DeLand
***Univ. of Central Florida, Orlando
Univ. of Florida, Gainesville
Univ. of Miami, Coral Gables
***Univ. of North Florida, Jacksonville
***Univ. of South Florida-St. Petersburg, St. Petersburg
Univ. of South Florida, Tampa
Univ. of Tampa, Tampa
***Univ. of West Florida, Pensacola

GEORGIA
***Albany State College, Albany
***Armstrong State College, Savannah
Augusta State College, Augusta
***Berry College, Mount Berry
Columbus College, Columbus
Fort Valley State College, Fort Valley
Georgia Institute of Technology, Atlanta
**Georgia Military College, Milledgeville
Georgia Southern College, Statesboro
***Georgia Southwestern College, Americus
Georgia State Univ., Atlanta
Mercer Univ., Macon
*North Georgia College, Dahlonega
Univ. of Georgia, Athens

GUAM
Univ. of Guam, Agana

HAWAII
Univ. of Hawaii, Honolulu

IDAHO
Boise State Univ., Boise
Idaho State Univ., Pocatello
Univ. of Idaho, Moscow

ILLINOIS
***Bradley Univ., Peoria
***Chicago State Univ., Chicago
Eastern Illinois Univ., Charleston
Illinois State Univ., Normal
Knox College, Galesburg
Loyola Univ. of Chicago, Chicago
Northern Illinois Univ., DeKalb
Southern Illinois Univ., Carbondale
Univ. of Illinois, Urbana-Champaign

Univ. of Illinois-Chicago Circle, Chicago
Western Illinois Univ., Macomb
Wheaton College, Wheaton

INDIANA
Ball State Univ., Muncie
Indiana Univ., Bloomington
Indiana Univ.-Purdue Univ. at Indianapolis, Indianapolis
***Indiana Univ.-Southeast, New Albany
Purdue Univ., West Lafayette
Rose-Hulman Institute of Technology, Terre Haute
Univ. of Notre Dame, Notre Dame

IOWA
***Drake Univ., Des Moines
Iowa State Univ. of S&T, Ames
***Univ. of Dubuque, Dubuque
Univ. of Iowa, Iowa City
***Univ. of Northern Iowa, Cedar Falls

KANSAS
***Emporia State Univ., Emporia
***Garden City Community College, Garden City
***Fort Hays State Univ., Fort Hays
Kansas State Univ. of A&AS, Manhattan
Pittsburg State Univ., Pittsburg
Univ. of Kansas, Lawrence
Wichita State Univ., Wichita

KENTUCKY
***Cumberland College, Williamsburg
Eastern Kentucky Univ., Richmond
***Kentucky State Univ., Frankfort
Morehead State Univ., Morehead
Murray State Univ., Murray
***Northern Kentucky Univ., Highland Heights
Univ. of Kentucky, Lexington
Univ. of Louisville, Louisville
Western Kentucky Univ., Bowling Green

LOUISIANA
***Centenary College of Louisiana, Shreveport
***Dillard Univ., New Orleans
***Grambling State Univ., Grambling
***Louisiana College, Pineville
***Louisiana State Univ. at Alexandria, Alexandria
Louisiana State Univ. and A&M College, Baton Rouge
***Louisiana State Univ. at Shreveport, Shreveport
Loyola Univ., New Orleans
McNeese State Univ., Lake Charles

NEBRASKA
Creighton Univ., Omaha
Kearney State College, Kearney

Univ. of Nebraska, Lincoln
***Univ. of Nebraska-Omaha, Omaha

NEVADA
Univ. of Nevada-Las Vegas, Las Vegas
Univ. of Nevada, Reno

NEW HAMPSHIRE
Univ. of New Hampshire, Durham

NEW JERSEY
***Jersey City State College, Jersey City
***Monmouth College, West Long Beach
Princeton Univ., Princeton
Rider College, Lawrenceville
Rutgers Univ., New Brunswick
Seton Hall Univ., South Orange
St. Peter's College, Jersey City

NEW MEXICO
Eastern New Mexico Univ., Portales
**New Mexico Military Institute, Roswell
New Mexico State Univ., Las Cruces
***Univ. of Albuquerque, Albuquerque

NEW YORK
Canisius College, Buffalo
Clarkson College of Technology, Potsdam
Cornell Univ., Ithaca
Fordham Univ., Bronx
Hofstra Univ., Hempstead
***John Jay College of Criminal Justice, City Univ. of New York, New York City
Niagara Univ., Niagara University
Polytechnic Institute of New York, Brooklyn
Rensselaer Polytechnic Institute, Troy
Rochester Institute of Technology, Rochester
Siena College, Loudonville
St. Bonaventure Univ., St. Bonaventure
St. Johns Univ., Jamaica
St. Lawrence Univ., Canton
***State Univ. of New York at Albany, Albany
State Univ. of New York at Brockport, Brockport
***State Univ. of New York at Cortland, Cortland
State Univ. of New York at Fredonia, Fredonia
***State Univ. of New York at Oswego, Oswego
Syracuse Univ., Syracuse

NORTH CAROLINA
Appalachian State Univ., Boone
Campbell Univ., Buies Creek
Davidson College, Davidson
Duke Univ., Durham
***East Carolina Univ., Greenville
***Elizabeth City State Univ., Elizabeth City

***Elon College, Elon College
North Carolina A&T State Univ., Greensboro
North Carolina State Univ. at Raleigh, Raleigh
St. Augustine's College, Raleigh
***Univ. of North Carolina at Charlotte, Charlotte
***Univ. of North Carolina at Wilmington, Wilmington
Wake Forest Univ., Winston-Salem
Western Carolina Univ., Cullowhee

NORTH DAKOTA
North Dakota State Univ. of A&AS, Fargo
Univ. of North Dakota, Grand Forks

OHIO
Bowling Green State Univ., Bowling Green
Central State Univ., Wilberforce
***Franklin Univ., Columbus
John Carroll Univ., Cleveland
Kent State Univ., Kent
Ohio State Univ., Columbus
Ohio Univ., Athens
***Rio Grande College, Rio Grande
Univ. of Akron, Akron
Univ. of Cincinnati, Cincinnati
Univ. of Dayton, Dayton
Univ. of Toledo, Toledo
***Wright State Univ., Dayton
Xavier Univ., Cincinnati
Youngstown State Univ., Youngstown

OKLAHOMA
Cameron Univ., Lawton
Central State Univ., Edmond
East Central Oklahoma State Univ., Ada
***Northeast Oklahoma State Univ. at Tahlequah, Tahlequah
Northwestern Oklahoma State Univ., Alva
***Oklahoma Panhandle State Univ., Goodwell
Oklahoma State Univ., Stillwater
Southwestern Oklahoma State Univ., Weatherford
Univ. of Oklahoma, Norman
***Univ. of Tulsa, Tulsa

OREGON
***Eastern Oregon State College, LaGrande
***Oregon Institute of Technology, Klamath Falls
Oregon State Univ., Corvallis
***Portland State Univ., Portland
Univ. of Oregon, Eugene

PENNSYLVANIA
***Altoona Campus, Penn State Univ., Altoona
***Behrend College, Penn State Univ., Erie
Bucknell Univ., Lewisburg

***California Univ. of Pennsylvania, California
    Carnegie-Mellon Univ., Pittsburgh
    Clarion Univ. of Pennsylvania, Clarion
***Delaware County Campus, Penn State Univ., Media
    Dickinson College, Carlisle
    Drexel Univ., Philadelphia
    Duquesne Univ., Pittsburgh
***East Stroudsburg Univ. of Pennsylvania, East Stroudsburg
    Gannon Univ., Erie
    Gettysburg College, Gettysburg
***Hazelton Campus, Penn State Univ., Hazelton
    Indiana Univ. of Pennsylvania, Indiana
    Lafayette College, Easton
    LaSalle College, Philadelphia
    Lehigh Univ., Bethlehem
***Lock Haven Univ. of Pennsylvania, Lock Haven
***Mansfield Univ. of Pennsylvania, Mansfield
***Millersville Univ. of Pennsylvania, Millersville
***Ogontz Campus, Penn State Univ., Abington
    Pennsylvania State Univ., University Park
***Schuylkill Campus, Penn State Univ., Schuylkill Haven
    Shippensburg Univ. of Pennsylvania, Shippensburg
***Slippery Rock Univ. of Pennsylvania, Slippery Rock
    Temple Univ., Philadelphia
    Univ. of Pennsylvania, Philadelphia
    Univ. of Pittsburgh, Pittsburgh
    Univ. of Scranton, Scranton
  **Valley Forge Military Academy and Junior College, Wayne
    Washington and Jefferson College, Washington
    Widener College, Chester

PUERTO RICO
    Univ. of Puerto Rico, Mayaguez Campus, Mayaguez
    Univ. of Puerto Rico, Rio Piedras Campus, Rio Piedras

RHODE ISLAND
***Bryant College, Smithfield Providence College, Providence
***Rhode Island College, Providence
    Univ. of Rhode Island, Kingston

SOUTH CAROLINA
***Benedict College, Columbia
    Clemson Univ., Clemson
***Erskine College & Seminary, Due West
***Francis Marion College, Florence
    Furman Univ., Greenville
    Presbyterian College, Clinton
    South Carolina State College, Orangeburg
  *The Citadel, Charleston
    Univ. of South Carolina, Columbia
    Wofford College, Spartanburg

SOUTH DAKOTA
***Black Hills State College, Spearfish
***Northern State College, Aberdeen
    South Dakota School of Mines and Technology, Rapid City
    South Dakota State Univ., Brookings
    Univ. of South Dakota, Vermillion

TENNESSEE
    Austin-Peay State Univ., Clarksville
    Carson-Newman College, Jefferson City
    East Tennessee State Univ., Johnson City
    Memphis State Univ., Memphis
    Middle Tennessee State Univ., Murfreesboro
    Tennessee Technological Univ., Cookeville
    Univ. of Tennessee, Knoxville
    Univ. of Tennessee at Chattanooga, Chattanooga
    Univ. of Tennessee at Martin, Martin
    Vanderbilt Univ., Nashville

TEXAS
    Bishop College, Dallas
    Hardin-Simmons Univ., Abilene
***Howard Payne Univ., Brownwood
***Lamar Univ., Beaumont
    Midwestern State Univ., Wichita Falls
    Pan American Univ., Edinburg

    Prairie View A&M Univ., Prairie View
    Rice Univ., Houston
    Sam Houston State Univ., Huntsville
    Stephen F. Austin State Univ., Nacogdoches
    St. Mary's Univ., San Antonio
***Tarleton State Univ., Stephenville
    Texas A&I Univ., Kingsville
    Texas A&M Univ., College Station
    Texas Christian Univ., Fort Worth
***Texas College, Tyler
    Texas Tech Univ., Lubbock
***Texas Woman's Univ., Denton
    Trinity Univ., San Antonio
    Univ. of Houston, Houston
    Univ. of Texas at Arlington, Arlington
    Univ. of Texas at Austin, Austin
    Univ. of Texas at El Paso, El Paso
    Univ. of Texas at San Antonio, San Antonio
    West Texas State Univ., Canyon

UTAH
    Brigham Young Univ., Provo
    Univ. of Utah, Salt Lake City
    Utah State Univ., Logan
    Weber State College, Ogden

VERMONT
  *Norwich Univ., Northfield
  Univ. of Vermont, Burlington

VIRGINIA
***Christopher Newport College, Newport News
***George Mason Univ., Fairfax
  Hampton Institute, Hampton
  James Madison Univ., Harrisonburg
***Longwood College, Farmville
***Lynchburg College, Lynchburg
  Norfolk State Univ., Norfolk
  Old Dominion Univ., Norfolk
  The College of William and Mary, Williamsburg
  Univ. of Richmond, Richmond
  Univ. of Virginia, Charlottesville
 *Virginia Military Institute, Lexington
  Virginia Polytechnic Institute and State Univ., Blacksburg
  Virginia State Univ., Petersburg
  Washington and Lee Univ., Lexington

WASHINGTON
***Central Washington Univ., Ellensburg
  Eastern Washington Univ., Cheney
  Gonzaga Univ., Spokane
  Seattle Univ., Seattle
  Univ. of Washington, Seattle
  Washington State Univ., Pullman

WEST VIRGINIA
  Marshall Univ., Huntington
  West Virginia State College, Institute
  West Virginia Univ., Morgantown

WISCONSIN
  Marquette Univ., Milwaukee
  Ripon College, Ripon
  St. Norbert College, DePere
  Univ. of Wisconsin-LaCrosse, LaCrosse
  Univ. of Wisconsin-Madison, Madison
  Univ. of Wisconsin-Milwaukee, Milwaukee
  Univ. of Wisconsin-Oshkosh, Oshkosh
  Univ. of Wisconsin-Platteville, Platteville
  Univ. of Wisconsin-Stevens Point, Stevens Point
  Univ. of Wisconsin-Whitewater, Whitewater

WYOMING
  Univ. of Wyoming, Laramie

  *Military College or University
 **Military Junior College
***Extension Center

AIR FORCE ROTC COLLEGES AND UNIVERSITIES

Some Air Force ROTC detachments have cross-enrollments with other colleges and universities—these are designated with a "+." Other schools listed below offer GMC or POC only. Also, some host schools are marked with "*" offering a Four-Year Program only and "**" offering a Two-Year Program only.

ALABAMA
  005 Auburn University, Auburn 36849
  010 University of Alabama, University 35486
  012 Samford University, Birmingham 35209
       + Birmingham Southern College, Birmingham 35204
       + Jefferson State Jr College, Birmingham 35215 (GMC only)
       + Lawson State Community College, Birmingham 35221 (GMC only)
       + Miles College, Birmingham 35208
       + University of Alabama in Birmingham, Birmingham 35294
       + University of Montevallo, Montevallo 35115
  015 Tuskegee Institute, Tuskegee 36088
  017 Troy State University, Troy 36082
  019 Alabama State University, Montgomery 36195
       + Auburn University at Montgomery, Montgomery 36117
       + Huntingdon College, Montgomery 36106
       + Troy State University in Montgomery, Montgomery 36104

ARIZONA
  020 University of Arizona, Tucson 85721
       + Pima Community College, Tucson 85709 (GMC only)
  025 Arizona State University, Tempe 85281
       + Glendale Community College, Glendale 85302 (GMC only)
       + Grand Canyon College, Phoenix 85017
       + Mesa Community College, Mesa 85202 (GMC only)
       + Phoenix College, Phoenix 85013 (GMC only)
       + Scottsdale Community College, Scottsdale 85252 (GMC only)
  027 Northern Arizona University, Flagstaff 86011
 027A Embry-Riddle Aeronautical at Prescott, Prescott 86302
       + Yavapai College, Prescott 86301 (GMC only)

ARKANSAS
  030 University of Arkansas, Fayetteville 72701

CALIFORNIA
  035 California State University, Fresno 93740
       + College of the Sequoias, Visalia 93277 (GMC only)
       + Fresno City College, Fresno 93741 (GMC only)
       + Merced College, Merced 95340 (GMC only)
       + Kings River College, Reedley 93654 (GMC only)
       + West Coast Bible College, Fresno 93710
       + West Hills College, Coalinga 93210 (GMC only)
  045 San Jose State University, San Jose 95192
       + Cabrillo College, Aptos 95003 (GMC only)

+ DeAnza College, Cupertino 95014 (GMC only)
+ Evergreen Valley College, San Jose 95135 (GMC only)
+ Foothill College, Los Altos Hills 94022 (GMC only)
+ Mission College, Santa Clara 95054 (GMC only)
+ Ohlone College, Fremont 94538 (GMC only)
+ San Jose City College, 2001 Moor Park Ave, San Jose 95128
+ Stanford University, San Jose 94305
+ University of Santa Clara, Santa Clara 95053
+ West Valley College, Saratoga 95070 (GMC only)
+ West Valley Joint Community College District, Saratoga 95070 (GMC only)

055   University of California at Los Angeles, Los Angeles 90024
+ California Lutheran College, Thousand Oaks 91360
+ California State College, San Bernardino 92407
+ California State University, Dominguez Hills 90747
+ California State Polytech University at Pomona, Pomona 91768
+ California State University at Fullerton, Fullerton 92634
+ California State University Long Beach, Long Beach 90840
+ California State University at Los Angeles, Los Angeles 90032
+ California State University at Northridge, Northridge 91330
+ Los Angeles Mission College, San Fernando 91340 (GMC only)
+ Mount St Mary's College, Los Angeles 90049 (GMC only)
+ Northrop University, Inglewood 90306
+ Santa Monica College, Santa Monica 90405 (GMC only)
+ Southern Illinois University, Sunnymead 92388
+ University of California Irvine, Irvine 92717
+ University of California Riverside, Riverside 92521
+ University of LaVerne, LaVerne 91750
+ University of California Santa Barbara, Santa Barbara 93106

055A   Loyola Marymount University, Los Angeles 90045
+ Antelope Valley College, Lancaster 93534 (GMC only)
+ California State University, Dominguez Hills 90747
+ California State University Long Beach, Long Beach 90840
+ California State College, San Bernardino 92407
+ California State Polytech University at Pomona, Pomona 91768
+ California State University at Los Angeles, Los Angeles 90032
+ California State University at Fullerton, Fullerton 92634
+ California State University at Northridge, Northridge 91330
+ Cypress College, Cypress 90630 (GMC only)
+ Chapman College, Orange 92666
+ East Los Angeles College, Monterey Park 91754 (GMC only)
+ El Camino College, Torrance 90506 (GMC only)
+ Fullerton College, Fullerton 92634 (GMC only)
+ Golden West College, Huntington Beach 92647 (GMC only)
+ Los Angeles City College, Los Angeles 90029 (GMC only)
+ Los Angeles Harbor College, Wilmington 90744 (GMC only)
+ Los Angeles Pierce College, Woodland Hills 91371 (GMC only)
+ Los Angeles Southwest College, Los Angeles 90047 (GMC only)
+ Los Angeles Trade Tech College, Los Angeles 90015 (GMC only)
+ Los Angeles Valley College, Van Nuys 91401 (GMC only)
+ Marymount Palos Verdes College, Rancho Palos Verdes 90274 (GMC only)

+ Moorpark College, Moorpark 93021 (GMC only)
+ Mount St Mary's College, Los Angeles 90049 (GMC only)
+ Mount San Jacinto College, San Jacinto 92383 (GMC only)
+ Northrop University, Inglewood 90306
+ Orange Coast College, Costa Mesa 92626 (GMC only)
+ Pasadena City College, Pasadena 91106 (GMC only)
+ Pepperdine University, Malibu 90265
+ Rio Hondo College, Whittier 90608 (GMC only)
+ Riverside City College, Riverside 92506 (GMC only)
+ Saddleback Community College, Mission Viejo 92675 (GMC only)
+ San Bernardino Valley College, San Bernardino 92403 (GMC only)
+ Santa Ana College, Santa Ana 92706 (GMC only)
+ Santa Monica College, Santa Monica 90405 (GMC only)
+ University of California Irvine, Irvine 92717
+ University of California Riverside, Riverside 92521
+ University of Redlands, Redlands 92373
+ Victor Valley College, Victorville 92403 (GMC only)
+ West Los Angeles College, Culver City 90230 (GMC only)
+ Westmont College, Santa Barbara 93108

055B   California State University at Long Beach, Long Beach 90503
+ California State College, San Bernardino 92407
+ California State University, Dominguez Hills, Carson 90747
+ California State University at Fullerton, Fullerton 92634
+ California State University Los Angeles, Los Angeles 90032
+ California State Polytech University at Pomona, Pomona 91768
+ Citrus College, Azusa 91702 (GMC only)
+ Chaffey College, Alta Loma 91702 (GMC only)
+ Cypress College, Cypress 90630 (GMC only)
+ El Camino College, Torrance 90506 (GMC only)
+ Fullerton College, Fullerton 92634 (GMC only)
+ Golden West College, Huntington Beach 92647 (GMC only)
+ Long Beach City College, Long Beach 90808 (GMC only)
+ Los Angeles Harbor College, Wilmington 90744 (GMC only)
+ Mount San Jacinto College, San Jacinto 92383 (GMC only)
+ Orange Coast College, Costa Mesa 92626 (GMC only)
+ Pasadena City College, Pasadena 91106 (GMC only)
+ Rio Hondo College, Whittier 90608 (GMC only)
+ Riverside City College, Riverside 92506 (GMC only)
+ Saddleback Community College, Mission Viejo 92675 (GMC only)
+ San Bernardino Valley College, 92403 (GMC only)
+ Santa Ana College, Santa Ana 92706 (GMC only)
+ University of California Riverside, Riverside 92521

060   University of Southern California, Los Angeles 90089
+ Biola College, La Mirada 90639
+ California Institute of Technology, Pasadena 91125 (POC only)
+ California Lutheran College, Thousand Oaks 91360
+ California State College, San Bernardino 92407
+ California State Polytech University at Pomona, Pomona 91768
+ California State University, Dominguez Hills 90747
+ California State University at Fullerton, Fullerton 92634
+ California State University at Los Angeles, Los Angeles 90032

+ California State University at Northridge, Northridge 91324
+ Chaffey College, Alta Loma 91701 (GMC only)
+ Chapman College, Orange 92666
+ Citrus College, Azusa 91701 (GMC only)
+ Claremont Men's College, Claremont 91711
+ Compton Community College, Compton 90221 (GMC only)
+ Cypress College, Cypress 90630 (GMC only)
+ East Los Angeles College, Monterey Park 91754 (GMC only)
+ El Camino College, Torrance 90506 (GMC only)
+ Fullerton College, Fullerton 92634 (GMC only)
+ Glendale Community College, Glendale 91208 (GMC only)
+ Golden West College, Huntington Beach 92647 (GMC only)
+ Harvey Mudd College, Claremont 91711
+ Long Beach City College, Long Beach 90808 (GMC only)
+ Los Angeles City College, Los Angeles 90029 (GMC only)
+ Los Angeles Harbor College, Wilmington 90744 (GMC only)
+ Los Angeles Pierce College, Woodland Hills 91371 (GMC only)
+ Los Angeles SW College, Los Angeles 90047 (GMC only)
+ Los Angeles Trade Tech College, Los Angeles 90015 (GMC only)
+ Los Angeles Valley College, Van Nuys 91401 (GMC only)
+ Moorpark College, Moorpark 93021 (GMC only)
+ Mt San Antonio College, Walnut 91789 (GMC only)
+ Northrop University, Inglewood 90306
+ Occidental College, Los Angeles 90041
+ Orange Coast College, Costa Mesa 92626 (GMC only)
+ Pasadena City College, Pasadena 91106 (GMC only)
+ Pepperdine University, Malibu 90265
+ Pomona College, Claremont 91711
+ Rio Hondo College, Whittier 90608 (GMC only)
+ San Bernardino Valley College, San Bernardino 92403 (GMC only)
+ University of California, Irvine 92717
+ University of California Riverside, Riverside 92521
+ Ventura College, Ventura 93003 (GMC only)
+ West Los Angeles College, Culver City 90230 (GMC only)
+ Whittier College, Whittier 90608
075 San Diego State University, San Diego 92182
+ Cuyamaca Community College, El Cajon 92020 (GMC only)
+ Grossmont Community College, El Cajon 92020 (GMC only)
+ San Diego Community College-City College, San Diego 92101 (GMC only)
+ San Diego Community College-Evening College, San Diego 92101 (GMC only)
+ San Diego Community College-Mesa College, San Diego 92111 (GMC only)
+ San Diego Community College-Miramar College, San Diego 92126 (GMC only)
+ Palomar College, San Marcos 92069 (GMC only)
+ Point Loma College, San Diego 92106
+ Southwestern College, Chula Vista 92010
+ University of California San Diego, La Jolla 92093
+ University of San Diego, San Diego 92110

**080 San Francisco State University, San Francisco 94132
+ Cogswell College, San Francisco 94108
+ Dominican College of San Rafael, San Rafael 94901
+ Golden Gate University, San Francisco 94105
+ University of California, Hastings College of Law, San Francisco 94102
+ University of California, San Francisco, Medical Center, San Francisco 94143
+ University of San Francisco, San Francisco 94117
085 University of California at Berkeley, Berkeley 94720
+ California State University at Hayward, Hayward 94542
+ Chabot College, Hayward 94545 (GMC only)
+ City College of San Francisco, San Francisco 94112
+ College of Alameda, Alameda 94501 (GMC only)
+ Contra Costa College, San Pablo 94806 (GMC only)
+ Diablo Valley College, Pleasant Hill 94523 (GMC only)
+ Graduate Theological Union, Berkeley 94709
+ Holy Names College, Oakland 94619
+ Laney College, Oakland 94619 (GMC only)
+ Los Medanos College, Pittsburg 94565 (GMC only)
+ Merritt College, Oakland 94619 (GMC only)
+ Mills College, Oakland 94613
+ Ohlone College, Fremont 94538
+ Sonoma State College, Rohnert Park 94928
+ St Mary's College, Moraga 94575
085A California State University at Sacramento, Sacramento 95819
+ American River College, Sacramento 95841
+ Butte Jr College, Oroville 95968 (GMC only)
+ Consumnes River College, Sacramento 95823
+ Sacramento City College, Sacramento 95822
+ Sierra College, Rocklin 95677
+ Solana Junior College, Fairfield 94533
+ University of California at Davis, Davis 95616
+ University of Pacific, Stockton 95211
+ Yuba College, Marysville 95901

COLORADO
090 Colorado State University, Fort Collins 80523
100 University of Northern Colorado, Greeley 80639
+ Aims Community College, Greeley 80631 (GMC only)
105 University of Colorado, Boulder 80309
+ Arapahoe Community College, Littleton 80120 (GMC only)
+ Colorado School of Mines, Golden 80401
+ Metropolitan State College, Denver 80204
+ Regis College, Denver 80221
+ University of Colorado at Denver, Denver 80202
+ University of Colorado Health Sciences Center, Denver 80202
+ University of Denver, Denver 80208

CONNECTICUT
115 University of Connecticut, Storrs 06268
+ Central Connecticut State, New Britain 06050
+ Eastern Connecticut State, Willimantic 06226

+ Southern Connecticut State, New Haven 06515
+ Trinity College, Hartford 06106
+ Western Connecticut State College, Danbury 06810
+ University of Hartford, West Hartford 06117

DELAWARE
128 University of Delaware, Newark 19716
+ Wilmington College, New Castle 19720

DISTRICT OF COLUMBIA
130 Howard University, Washington 20059
+ American University, Washington 20016
+ Georgetown University, Washington 20057
+ George Washington University, Washington 20052
+ The Catholic University of America, Washington 20064
+ Trinity College, Washington 20017
+ University of the District of Columbia, Mt Vernon Square, Washington 20005

FLORIDA
145 Florida State University, Tallahassee 32306
+ Florida A&M University, Tallahassee 32307
+ Tallahassee Community College, Tallahassee 32304 (GMC only)
150 University of Florida, Gainesville 32611
+ Santa Fe Community College, Gainesville 32602 (GMC only)
155 University of Miami, Coral Gables 33124
+ Barry College, Miami 33161
+ Biscayne College, Miami 33054
+ Florida International University, Miami 33199 (GMC only)
+ Florida Memorial College, Miami 33054
+ Miami-Dade Community College, Miami 33176 (GMC only)
157 Embry-Riddle Aeronautical University, Daytona Beach 32015
+ Bethune-Cookman College, Daytona Beach 32015
+ Daytona Beach Community College, Daytona Beach 32015 (GMC only)
+ University of Central Florida, Daytona Center 32014
158 University of South Florida, Tampa 33620
+ Hillborough Community College, Tampa 33622 (GMC only)
+ Pasco-Hernando Community College, Dade City 33535 (GMC only)
+ Polk Community College, Winter Haven 33880 (GMC only)
+ St Leo College, Saint Leo 33753
+ St Petersburg Jr College, Saint Petersburg 33733 (GMC only)
+ University of Tampa, Tampa 33606
159 University of Central Florida, Orlando 32816
+ Brevard Community College, Cocoa 32922 (GMC only)
+ Florida Southern College, McCoy Campus, Orlando 32812
+ Lake-Sumter Community College, Leesburg 32748 (GMC only)
+ Rollins College, Winter Park 32789
+ Seminole Community College, Sanford 32771 (GMC only)
+ Valencia Community College, Orlando 32802 (GMC only)

GEORGIA
160 University of Georgia, Athens 30602
+ Medical College of Georgia, Augusta 30901

165   Georgia Institute of Technology, Atlanta 30332
    + Agnes Scott College, Decatur 30030
    + Clark College, Atlanta 30314
    + Southern Tech Institute, Marietta 30060
    + Georgia State University, Atlanta 30314
    + Morehouse College, Atlanta 30314
    + Morris Brown College, Atlanta 30314
    + Spelman College, Atlanta 30314
172   Valdosta State College, Valdosta 31698

HAWAII
175   University of Hawaii at Manoa, Honolulu 96822
    + Chaminade University of Honolulu, Honolulu 96816
    + Kapiolani Community College, Honolulu 96814 (GMC only)
    + Leeward Community College, Pearl City 96782 (GMC only)
    + Windward Community College, Kaneohe 96744 (GMC only)
    + Honolulu Community College, Honolulu 96814
    + Hawaii Pacific College, Honolulu 96814
    + West Oahu College, Pearl City 96782

ILLINOIS
190   University of Illinois, Urbana 61820
    + Parkland College, Champaign 61820 (GMC only)
195   Illinois Institute of Technology, Chicago 60616
    + Chicago State University, Chicago 60628
    + Richard J. Daley College, Chicago 60652 (GMC only)
    + Elmhurst College, Elmhurst 60126
    + Governors State University, Park Forest South 60466
    + John Marshall Law School, Chicago 60604
    + Kennedy-King College, Chicago 60621 (GMC only)
    + Lewis University, Lockport 60441
    + Loop College, Chicago 60601 (GMC only)
    + Malcolm X College, Chicago 60612 (GMC only)
    + North Central College, Naperville 60566
    + Northern Illinois University, DeKalb 60115
    + Northeastern Illinois University, Chicago 60625
    + Northwestern University, Evanston 60201
    + Olive-Harvey College, Chicago 60628 (GMC only)
    + Rush University, Chicago 60612
    + St Xavier College, Chicago 60655
    + Triton College, River Grove 60171 (GMC only)
    + Truman College, Chicago 60640 (GMC only)
    + University of Illinois at Chicago Circle, Chicago 60680
    + University of Illinois Medical Center at Chicago, Chicago 60680
    + Wright College, Chicago 60634 (GMC only)
205   Southern Illinois University, Carbondale 62901
206   Southern Illinois University at Edwardsville, Edwardsville 62026
    + Belleville Area College, Belleville 62221 (GMC only)
    + Lewis and Clark Community College, Godfrey 62035 (GMC only)
    + McKendree College, Lebanon 62254
207   Parks College of St Louis University, Cahokia 62206
    + Harris Stowe State College, St Louis, MO 63103

+ St Louis University, St Louis, MO 63103
+ University of Missouri at St Louis, St Louis, MO 63121
+ Washington University, St Louis, MO 63130
+ St Louis Community College, St Louis, MO 63110 (GMC only)

INDIANA
215 Indiana University, Bloomington 47401
+ Butler University, Indianapolis 46208
+ DePauw University, Greencastle 46135
+ Indiana State University, Terre Haute 47809
+ Indiana University-Purdue University at Indianapolis, Indianapolis 46202
+ Marian College, Indianapolis 46222
+ Rose-Hulman Institute of Technology, Terre Haute 47803
220 Purdue University, Lafayette 47907
225 University of Notre Dame, Notre Dame 46556
+ Holy Cross Jr College, Notre Dame 46556 (GMC only)
+ Indiana University at South Bend, South Bend 46544
+ St Mary's College, Notre Dame 46556

IOWA
250 Iowa State University, Ames 50011
+ Drake University, Des Moines 50311
255 University of Iowa, Iowa City 52242

KANSAS
270 Kansas State University, Manhattan 66506
280 The University of Kansas, Lawrence 66045
+ Washburn University, Topeka 66621

KENTUCKY
290 University of Kentucky, Lexington 40506
+ Georgetown College, Georgetown 40324
+ Kentucky State University, Frankfort 40601
+ Midway College, Midway 40347 (GMC only)
+ Transylvania University, Lexington 40508
295 University of Louisville, Louisville 40292
+ Bellarmine College, Louisville 40205
+ Indiana University Southeast, New Albany 47150
+ Louisville Presbyterian Theological Seminary, Louisville 40205
+ Southern Baptist Theological Seminary, Louisville 40206
+ Spalding College, Louisville 40203

LOUISIANA
305 Louisiana Tech University, Ruston 71272
310 Louisiana State University and A&M College, Baton Rouge 70892
+ Southern University A&M College, Baton Rouge 70813
311 Grambling State University, Grambling 71245
315 University of Southwestern Louisiana, Lafayette 70504
320 University of New Orleans, New Orleans 70122
+ Dillard University, New Orleans 70122
+ Louisiana State University School of Nursing, New Orleans 70119
+ Loyola University in New Orleans, New Orleans 70118
+ Our Lady of Holy Cross College, New Orleans 70114

+ Southern University of New Orleans, New Orleans 70126
+ Tulane University, New Orleans 70118
+ Xavier University of Louisiana, New Orleans 70125

MAINE
326   University of Maine at Orono 04469
+ Husson College, Bangor 04401

MARYLAND
330   University of Maryland, College Park 20742
+ Bowie State College, Bowie 20715
+ George Mason University, Fairfax VA 22030
+ Johns Hopkins University, Baltimore 21218
+ Loyola College, Baltimore 21210
+ Shepherd College, Shepherdstown WV 25443
+ Towson State University, Baltimore 21204
+ Western Maryland College, Westminster 21157

MASSACHUSETTS
340   College of the Holy Cross, Worcester 01610
+ Anna Maria College, Paxton 01612
+ Assumption College, Worcester 01609
+ Becker Jr College, Leicester 01524 (GMC only)
+ Becker Jr College, Worcester 01609 (GMC only)
+ Central New England College, Worcester 01608
+ Clark University, Worcester 01610
+ Quinsigamond Community College, Worcester 01606 (GMC only)
+ Worcester Polytechnic Institute, Worcester 01609
+ Worcester State College, Worcester 01602
345   University of Lowell, Lowell 01854
+ Bentley College, Waltham 02154
+ Daniel Webster College, Nashua NH 03060
+ Endicott College, Beverly 01915
+ Gordon College, Wenham 01984
+ Middlesex Community College, Bedford 01730 (GMC only)
+ New Hampshire College, Manchester NH 03104
+ New England College, Henniker NH 03204
+ Northern Essex Community College, Haverhill 01830 (GMC only)
+ North Shore Community College, Beverly 01915 (GMC only)
+ Notre Dame College, Manchester NH 03104
+ Rivier College, Nashua NH 03060
+ Salem State College, Salem 01970
+ St Anselm College, Manchester NH 03102
355   Boston University, Boston 02215
+ Northeastern University, Boston 02115
365   Massachusetts Institute of Technology, Cambridge 02139
+ Harvard University, Cambridge 02138
+ Tufts University, Medford 02155
+ Wellesley College, Wellesley 02181
370   University of Massachusetts, Amherst 01003
+ Amherst College, Amherst 01002
+ Mount Holyoke College, South Hadley 01075
+ Smith College, Northampton 01063
+ Western New England College, Springfield 01119

MICHIGAN
380   Michigan State University, East Lansing 48824
  + Lansing Community College, Lansing 48901 (GMC only)
390   The University of Michigan, Ann Arbor 49109
  + Concordia College, Ann Arbor 48105
  + Eastern Michigan University, Ypsilanti 48197
  + Lawrence Institute of Technology, Southfield 48075
  + University of Michigan at Dearborn, Dearborn 48128
  + Wayne State University, Detroit 48202 (POC only)
400   Michigan Technological University, Houghton 49931
  + Suomi College, Hancock 49930 (GMC only)

MINNESOTA
410   The College of St Thomas, St Paul 55105
  + Bethel College, St Paul 55112
  + Anoka-Ramsey Community College, Coon Rapids 55433 (GMC only)
  + Augsburg College, Minneapolis 55454
  + College of St Catherine, St Paul 55105
  + Hamline University, St Paul 55104
  + Inver Hills Community College, Inver Grove Heights 55075 (GMC only)
  + Lakewood Community College, White Bear Lake 55110 (GMC only)
  + Macalester College, St Paul 55105
  + Normandale Community College, Bloomington 55431 (GMC only)
  + North Hennepin Community College, Minneapolis 55445 (GMC only)
  + William Mitchell College of Law, St Paul 55105
415   University of Minnesota, Minneapolis 55455
420   University of Minnesota at Duluth, Duluth 55812
  + College of St Scholastica, Duluth 55811

MISSISSIPPI
425   Mississippi State University, Mississippi State 39762
  + Mississippi University for Women, Columbus 39701
430   University of Mississippi, University 38677
430A Mississippi Valley State University, Itta Bena 38941
  + Delta State University, Cleveland 38732
432   University of Southern Mississippi, Hattiesburg 39401
  + William Carey College, Hattiesburg 39401

MISSOURI
437   Southeast Missouri State University, Cape Girardeau 63701
440   University of Missouri, Columbia 65211
  + Columbia College, Columbia 65201
  + Stephens College, Columbia 65201
  + William Woods College, Fulton 65251
440A University of Missouri-Rolla, Rolla 65401

MONTANA
450   Montana State University, Bozeman 59717

NEBRASKA
465   University of Nebraska, Lincoln 68588
  + Concordia Teachers College, Seward 68434
  + Nebraska Wesleyan University, Lincoln 68504
470   University of Nebraska at Omaha, Omaha 68182
  + Bellevue College, Bellevue 68005

+ College of St Mary, Omaha 68124
+ Creighton University, Omaha 68178
+ Iowa Western Community College, Council Bluffs, IA 51501 (GMC only)

NEW HAMPSHIRE
475   University of New Hampshire, Durham 03824
+ Nathaniel Hawthorne College, Antrim 03440
+ New England College, Henniker 03242
+ New Hampshire College, Manchester 03104
+ St Anselm's College, Manchester 03102
+ The University of Southern Maine, Portland ME 04103
+ University of New Hampshire, Plymouth State College, Plymouth 03264

NEW JERSEY
485   Rutgers, The State University, New Brunswick 08901
+ Brookdale Community College, Lincroft 07738 (GMC only)
+ Mercer County Community College, Trenton 08690 (GMC only)
+ Middlesex County College, Edison 08817 (GMC only)
+ Monmouth College, West Long Beach 07764
+ Princeton University, Princeton 08540
+ Rider College, Trenton 08648
+ Rutgers University, Camden Campus 08102
+ Somerset County College, Somerville 08876 (GMC only)
+ Trenton State College, Trenton 08625
+ Union College, Cranford 07016 (GMC only)
+ Wagner College, Staten Island NY 10301
490   New Jersey Institute of Technology, Newark 07102
+ Essex County Community College, Newark 07102 (GMC only)
+ Fairleigh Dickinson University-Teaneck, Teaneck 07666
+ Jersey City State College, Jersey City 07305
+ Kean College of New Jersey, Union 07083
+ Montclair State College, Upper Montclair 07043
+ Rutgers University, Newark Campus 07102
+ Seton Hall University, South Orange 07079
+ Stevens Institute of Technology, Hoboken 07030
+ St Peter's College, Jersey City 07306
+ William Paterson College of New Jersey, Wayne 07470

NEW MEXICO
505   New Mexico State University, Las Cruces 88003
+ University of Texas at El Paso, El Paso TX 79968
510   University of New Mexico, Albuquerque 87131
+ University of Albuquerque, Albuquerque 87140

NEW YORK
520   Cornell University, Ithaca 14853
+ Ithaca College, Ithaca 14850
+ SUNY at Cortland, Cortland 13045
+ Tompkins Cortland Community College, Dryden 13053 (GMC only)
+ Wells College, Aurora 13056
535   Syracuse University, Syracuse 13210
+ LeMoyne College, Syracuse 13214

+ New School for Social Research, New York 10011
+ Onondaga Community College, Syracuse 13215 (GMC only)
+ SUNY, College of Environmental Science & Forestry, Syracuse 13210
+ Utica College of Syracuse University, Utica 13502
536   Clarkson College of Technology, Potsdam 13676
+ State University of New York at Potsdam, Potsdam 13676
+ St Lawrence University, Canton 13617
+ State University Agriculture and Tech College at Canton, Canton 13617 (GMC only)
550   Rensselaer Polytechnic Institute, Troy 12181
+ Albany College of Pharmacy, Albany 12208
+ College of St Rose, Albany 12203
+ Fulton/Montgomery Community College, Johnstown 12095 (GMC only)
+ Hudson Valley Community College, Troy 12180 (GMC only)
+ Maria College, Albany 12208 (GMC only)
+ Russell Sage College, Troy 12180
+ Schenectady County Community College, Schenectady 12305 (GMC only)
+ Siena College, Loudonville 12211
+ Skidmore College, Saratoga Springs 12866
+ State University of New York at Albany, Albany 12222
+ SUNY, Empire State College, Saratoga Springs 12866
+ Union College, Schenectady 12308
560   Manhattan College, Riverdale 10471
+ Academy of Aeronautics, Flushing 11371 (GMC only)
+ Adelphi University, Garden City 11530
+ College of Mount St Vincent, Riverdale 10471
+ Columbia University, New York 10027
+ Elizabeth Seton College, Yonkers 10701 (GMC only)
+ C.W. Post Center of Long Island University, Greenvale 11548
+ Long Island University Brooklyn Center, Brooklyn 11201
+ Mercy College, Dobbs Ferry 10522
+ Molloy College, Rockville Centre 11570
+ Nassau Community College, Garden City 11530 (GMC only)
+ New York Institute of Technology, Old Westbury 11568
+ Pace University, Pace Plaza, New York 10038
+ Polytechnic Institute of New York, Brooklyn 11201
+ St Francis College, Brooklyn 11201
+ St Joseph's College/Brentwood, Patchogue 11772
+ St Thomas Aquinas College, Sparkill 10976
+ Southampton Community College, Southampton 11968 (GMC only)
+ Suffolk Community College, Brentwood 11717 (GMC only)
+ SUNY, A&T Farmingdale, Farmingdale 11735 (GMC only)
+ SUNY, Old Westbury, Old Westbury 11568
+ SUNY, Stony Brook, Stony Brook 11794

NORTH CAROLINA
585   Duke University, Durham 27706
+ North Carolina Central University, Durham 27707
590   University of North Carolina, Chapel Hill 27514

590A University of North Carolina at Charlotte, Charlotte 28223
  + Barber-Scotia College, Belmont 28025
  + Belmont Abbey College, Belmont 28012
  + Central Piedmont Community College, Charlotte 28204 (GMC only)
  + Davidson College, Davidson 28036
  + Gaston College, Dallas 28034 (GMC only)
  + Johnson C. Smith University, Charlotte 28216
  + Sacred Heart College, Belmont 28012
  + Queens College, Charlotte 28274
  + Wingate College, Wingate 28174 (GMC only)
  + Winthrop College, Rock Hill 29733
595 North Carolina State University at Raleigh, Raleigh 27607
  + Meredith College, Raleigh 27611
  + Peace College, Raleigh 27604 (GMC only)
  + Shaw University, Raleigh 27611
  + St Augustine's College, Raleigh 27611
  + St Mary's College, Raleigh 27611 (GMC only)
600 East Carolina University, Greenville 27834
  + Pitt Community College, Greenville 27834 (GMC only)
605 North Carolina A&T State University, Greensboro 27411
  + Bennett College, Greensboro 27420
  + Greensboro College, Greensboro 27420
  + Guilford College, Greensboro 27410
  + High Point College, High Point 27262
  + University of North Carolina, Greensboro 27412
607 Fayetteville State University, Fayetteville 28301
  + Pembroke State University, Pembroke 28372

NORTH DAKOTA
610 North Dakota State University of A&AS, Fargo 58105
  + Concordia College, Moorhead MN 56560
  + Moorhead State University, Moorhead MN 56560

OHIO
620 Bowling Green State University, Bowling Green 43403
  + Ashland College, Ashland 44805
  + Defiance College, Defiance 43512
  + Findlay College, Findlay 45840
  + Heidelberg College, Tiffin 44883
  + Ohio Northern University, Ada 45810
  + University of Toledo, Toledo 43606
630 + Kent State University, Kent 44242
640 + Miami University, Oxford 45056
  + Miami University Hamilton Branch, Hamilton 45011 (GMC only)
  + Miami University, Middletown Branch, Middletown 45052 (GMC only)
643 Wright State University, Dayton 45435
  + Antioch College, Yellow Springs 45387
  + Central State University, Wilberforce 45384
  + Clark Technical College, Springfield 45505 (GMC only)
  + Cedarville College, Cedarville 45314
  + Edison State Community College, Piqua 45356 (GMC only)
  + Sinclair Community College, Dayton 45402 (GMC only)

+ Southern State Community College, Wilmington 45177 (GMC only)
+ University of Dayton, Dayton 45469
+ Urbana College, Urbana 43078
+ Wilberforce University, Wilberforce 45384
+ Wilmington College, Wilmington 45177
+ Wittenburg University, Springfield 45501
645 The Ohio State University, Columbus 43210
+ Capital University, Columbus 43209
+ Franklin University, Columbus 43215
+ Ohio Dominican College, Columbus 43219
+ Ohio Institute of Technology, Columbus 43219 (POC only)
+ Ohio Wesleyan University, Delaware 43015
+ Otterbein College, Westerville 43081
650 Ohio University, Athens 45701
660 The University of Akron, Akron 44325
665 University of Cincinnati, Cincinnati 45221
+ College of Mount St Joseph, Mount St Joseph 45051
+ Northern Kentucky University, Highland Heights KY 41075
+ Thomas More College, Fort Mitchell KY 41017
+ Xavier University, Cincinnati 45207
+ Edgecliff College, Cincinnati 45207
+ Cincinnati Tech College, Cincinnati 45225

OKLAHOMA
670 Oklahoma State University, Stillwater 74078
675 The University of Oklahoma, Norman 73019
+ Oklahoma City University, Oklahoma City 73106
+ Oklahoma Christian College, Oklahoma City 73111
+ Oscar Rose Jr College, Midwest City 73110 (GMC only)
+ St Gregory's College, Shawnee 74801 (GMC only)

OREGON
685 Oregon State University, Corvallis 97331
+ Linn-Benton Community College, Albany 97321 (GMC only)
+ Western Oregon State College, Monmouth 97361
+ University of Oregon, Eugene 97403
695 University of Portland, Portland 97203
+ Clackamas Community College, Oregon City 97203 (GMC only)
+ Clark College, Vancouver, Washington 98663 (GMC only)
+ Concordia College, Portland 97211
+ Mt Hood Community College, Gresham 97030 (GMC only)
+ Portland Community College, Portland 97219 (GMC only)
+ Portland State University, Portland 97207
+ Oregon Health Sciences Center, Portland 97201
+ Willamette University, Salem 97301
+ Warner-Pacific College, Portland 97215

PENNSYLVANIA
715 Lehigh University, Bethlehem 18015
+ Allentown College of St Francis de Sales, Center Valley 18034
+ Cedar Crest College, Allentown 18104
+ East Stroudsburg State College, East Stroudsburg 18301
+ Kutztown State College, Kutztown 19530

+ Lafayette College, Easton 18042
+ Lehigh County Community College, Schnecksville 18078 (GMC only)
+ Moravian College, Bethlehem 18018
+ Muhlenburg College, Allentown 18104
+ Northampton County Area Community College, Bethlehem 18017 (GMC only)
+ Pennsylvania State-Allentown, Fogelsville 18051
+ Pennsylvania State University Berks, Reading 29608 (GMC only)
720 The Pennsylvania State University, University Park 16802
730 University of Pittsburgh, Pittsburgh 15260
+ Community College of Allegheny County, Pittsburgh 15212 (GMC only)
+ Community College of Allegheny County, Boyce County, Monroeville 15146 (GMC only)
+ Community College of Allegheny County, North Campus, Pittsburgh 15237 (GMC only)
+ Community College of Allegheny County, West Mifflin 15122 (GMC only)
+ Carlow College, Pittsburgh 15213
+ Chatham College, Pittsburgh 15232
+ Duquesne University, Pittsburgh 15282
+ La Roche College, Pittsburgh 15237
+ Point Park College, Pittsburgh 15222
+ Robert Morris College, Corapolis 15108
+ St Vincent College, Latrobe 15650
730A Carnegie-Mellon University, Pittsburgh 15213
745 Grove City College, Grove City 16127
+ Slippery Rock State College, Slippery Rock 26257
750 St Joseph's University, Philadelphia 19131
+ Drexel University, Philadelphia 19104
+ Eastern College, St Davids 19087
+ LaSalle College, Philadelphia 19141
+ Rutgers-Camden, Camden NJ 08102
+ Temple University, Philadelphia 19122
+ Thomas Jefferson University, Philadelphia 19107
+ University of Pennsylvania, Philadelphia 19104
+ Villanova University, Villanova 19085
+ West Chester State College, West Chester 19380
+ Widener University, Chester 19013
752 Wilkes College, Wilkes-Barre 18766
+ Bloomsburg State College, Bloomsburg 17815
+ College Misericordia, Dallas 18612
+ Keystone Jr College, La Plume 18440 (GMC only)
+ King's College, Wilkes-Barre 18711
+ Lackawanna Jr College, Scranton 18503 (GMC only)
+ Luzerne County Community College, Nanticoke 18634 (GMC only)
+ Marywood College, Scranton 18509
+ Pennsylvania State University, Hazelton Campus, Hazelton 18201 (GMC only)
+ Pennsylvania State University, Wilkes-Barre Campus, Wilkes-Barre 18708 (GMC only)
+ Pennsylvania State University, Worthington Scranton Campus,

Dunmore 18512 (GMC only)
+ The University of Scranton, Scranton 18510

PUERTO RICO
755 University of Puerto Rico, Rio Piedras, Rio Piedras 00936
+ Bayamon Central University, Bayamon 00619
+ Bayamon Regional College, Rio Piedras 00931
+ Inter American University, Hato Rey 00919
+ Sacred Heart University, Santurce 00914
+ University of Puerto Rico, Bayamon Technical University College, Bayamon 00936
+ University of Puerto Rico, Cardina Regional College, Carolina 00931
+ University of Puerto Rico, Cayey University College, Cayey 00633
+ University of Puerto Rico, Humacao University College, Humacao 00661
+ World University, Hato Rey 00917
756 University of Puerto Rico, Mayaguez 00709
+ Inter American University of Puerto Rico, San German 00753
+ University of Puerto Rico Aguadilla Regional College, Aguadilla 00603

SOUTH CAROLINA
*765 The Citadel, Charleston 29409
770 Clemson University, Clemson 29631
+ Anderson College, Anderson 29621 (GMC only)
+ Central Wesleyan College, Central 29630
+ Tri-County Tech. College, Pendleton 29670 (GMC only)
**772 Baptist College at Charleston, Charleston 29411
+ College of Charleston, Charleston 29401
+ Medical University of South Carolina, Charleston 29403
+ South Carolina State, Orangeburg 29117
775 University of South Carolina, Columbia 29208
+ Benedict College, Columbia 29204

SOUTH DAKOTA
780 South Dakota State University, Brookings 57007

TENNESSEE
785 Memphis State University, Memphis 38152
+ Christian Brothers College, Memphis 38104
+ LeMoyne-Owen College, Memphis 38126
+ Shelby State Community College, Memphis 38104 (GMC only)
+ Southwestern at Memphis, Memphis 38112
+ University of Tennessee Medical School, Memphis 38163
790 Tennessee State University, Nashville 37203
+ Aquinas Jr College, Nashville 37205 (GMC only)
+ Belmont College, Nashville 37203
+ David Lipscomb College, Nashville 37203
+ Fisk University, Nashville 37203
+ Meharry Medical College, Nashville 37208
+ Middle Tennessee State University, Murfreesboro 37130
+ Trevecca Nazarene College, Nashville 37210
+ Vanderbilt University, Nashville 37240
+ Volunteer State Community College, Gallatin 37066 (GMC only)

800   University of Tennessee, Knoxville 37996
      + Knoxville College, Knoxville 37921

TEXAS
805   Texas A&M University, College Station 77841
810   Baylor University, Waco 76798
      + University of Mary Hardin-Baylor, Belton 76513
      + McLennan Community College, Waco 76708 (GMC only)
      + Paul Quinn College, Waco 76704
820   Texas Tech University, Lubbock 79409
      + Lubbock Christian College, Lubbock 79407
825   The University of Texas at Austin, Austin 78712
      + Austin Community College, Austin 78767 (GMC only)
      + Concordia Lutheran College, Austin 78705
      + St Edward's University, Austin 78704
830   East Texas State University, Commerce 75428
835   North Texas State University, Denton 76203
      + Southern Methodist University, Dallas 75275
      + Texas Woman's University, Denton 76204
      + University of Dallas, Irving 75061
      + University of Texas at Dallas, Richardson 75080 (POC only)
840   Southwest Texas State University, San Marcos 78666
      + Texas Lutheran College, Seguin 78155
      + University of Texas at San Antonio, San Antonio 78285
845   Texas Christian University, Fort Worth 76129
      + Baylor School of Nursing, Dallas 75246
      + Tarrant County Jr College, Fort Worth 76102 (GMC only)
      + Texas Wesleyan College, Fort Worth 76105
      + University of Texas at Arlington, Arlington 76019
847   Angelo State University, San Angelo 76909

UTAH
850   University of Utah, Salt Lake City 84112
      + Weber State College, Ogden 84408
      + Westminster College, Salt Lake City 84105
855   Brigham Young University, Provo 84602
      + Utah Technical College, Provo 84601 (GMC only)
860   Utah State University, Logan 84322

VERMONT
865   St Michael's College, Winooski 05404
      + Champlain College, Burlington 05401 (GMC only)
      + Lyndon State College, Lyndonville 05851
      + Trinity College, Burlington 05401
      + University of Vermont & State Agricultural College, Burlington 05401
867   Norwich University, Northfield 05663

VIRGINIA
875   Virginia Polytechnic Institute, Blacksburg 24060
*880   Virginia Military Institute, Lexington 24450
890   University of Virginia, Charlottesville 22903
      + Piedmont Virginia Community College, Charlottesville 22901 (GMC only)

WASHINGTON
**895 Central Washington University, Ellensburg 98926
  900 University of Puget Sound, Tacoma 98416
    + Fort Steilacoom Community College, Tacoma 98498 (GMC only)
    + Pacific Lutheran University, Tacoma 98447
    + St Martin's College, Olympia 98503
    + Southern Illinois University at McChord AFB 98438
    + Tacoma Community College, Tacoma 98465 (GMC only)
  905 Washington State University, Pullman 99164
    + University of Idaho, Moscow, Idaho 83843
  910 University of Washington, Seattle 98195
    + Bellevue Community College, Bellevue 98007 (GMC only)
    + Everett Community College, Everett 98201 (GMC only)
    + Edmonds Community College, Lynwood 98036 (GMC only)
    + Green River Community College, Auburn 98002 (GMC only)
    + Highline Community College, Midway 98031 (GMC only)
    + North Seattle Community College, Seattle 98103 (GMC only)
    + Seattle Central Community College, Seattle 98122 (GMC only)
    + Seattle University, Seattle 98122
    + Shoreline Community College, Seattle 98133 (GMC only)
    + Seattle Community College, South Campus, Seattle 98106 (GMC only)

WEST VIRGINIA
  915 West Virginia University, Morgantown 26506
    + Fairmont State College, Fairmont 26554

WISCONSIN
  925 University of Wisconsin, Madison 53706
  930 University of Wisconsin at Superior, Superior 54880

WYOMING
  940 University of Wyoming, Laramie 82071

NAVAL ROTC COLLEGES AND UNIVERSITIES

A crosstown college/university is an institution linked by a formal written agreement with a host university and the NROTC unit. This permits students from the crosstown college to enroll in the NROTC program at the host institution. Four-year scholarship selectees normally attend only the host institutions, but may be considered for crosstown placement on a case-by-case basis.

State	NROTC Unit	Crosstown Colleges/Universities
Alabama	Auburn University Auburn, AL 36830	
Arizona	University of Arizona Tucson, AZ 85721	
California	University of California at Berkeley Berkeley, CA 94720	*California State University—Hayward, Sacramento, San Jose *San Francisco State University *San Jose State University Stanford University University of California—Davis University of San Francisco *University of Santa Clara
	University of California at Los Angeles (UCLA) Los Angeles, CA 90024	California State University—Fullerton, Long Beach, Los Angeles, Northridge Loyola Marymount University Northrop University Occidental College Pepperdine University University of California—Irvine
	University of San Diego and San Diego State University San Diego, CA 92110 (Consortium)	University of California—San Diego
	University of Southern California Los Angeles, CA 90007	California Institute of Technology California State Polytechnic University Claremont McKenna College Harvey Mudd College
Colorado	University of Colorado Boulder, CO 80309	
District of Columbia	George Washington University Washington, DC 20058	*American University *Catholic University of America *Georgetown University *Howard University *University of D.C. *University of Maryland
Florida	Florida A&M University Tallahassee, FL 32307	Florida State University Tallahassee Community College
	Jacksonville University Jacksonville, FL 32211	Edward Waters College Florida Junior College—Jacksonville University of North Florida

140

State	NROTC Unit	Crosstown Colleges/Universities
	University of Florida Gainesville, FL 32611	
Georgia	Georgia Institute of Technology (Georgia Tech) Atlanta, GA 30332	Agnes Scott College Clark College Georgia State University Kennesaw College Morehouse College Morris Brown College Oglethorpe University Southern Technical Institute Spelman College
	Savannah State College Savannah, GA 31404	Armstrong State College
Idaho	University of Idaho Moscow, ID 83843	Washington State University
Illinois	Illinois Institute of Technology (Illinois Tech) Chicago, IL 60616	Elmhurst College Prairie State College Purdue University—Calumet *University of Chicago University of Illinois—Chicago Wilbur Wright City College
	Northwestern University Evanston, IL 60201	Loyola University
	University of Illinois Champaign, IL 61820	Parkland College
Indiana	Purdue University West Lafayette, IN 47907	
	University of Notre Dame Notre Dame, IN 46556	Bethel College Indiana University—South Bend St. Mary's College
Iowa	Iowa State University Ames, IA 50010	
Kansas	University of Kansas Lawrence, KS 66045	
Louisiana	Southern University A&M Baton Rouge, LA 70813	Louisiana State University
	Tulane University New Orleans, LA 70118	
Maine	**Maine Maritime Academy Castine, ME 04421	*University of Maine—Orono
Massachusetts	Boston University Boston, MA 02215	Northeastern University
	College of the Holy Cross Worcester, MA 01610	Anna Maria College Assumption College Central New England College Clark University Worcester Polytechnic Institute Worcester State College
	Massachusetts Institute of Technology (MIT) Cambridge, MA 02139	*Harvard University Tufts University *Wellesley College

State	NROTC Unit	Crosstown Colleges/Universities
Michigan	University of Michigan Ann Arbor, MI 48104	Eastern Michigan University—Ypsilanti
Minnesota	University of Minnesota Minneapolis, MN 55455	Augsburg College College of St. Thomas Macalester College
Mississippi	University of Mississippi University, MS 38677	
Missouri	University of Missouri Columbia, MO 65201	Columbia College
Nebraska	University of Nebraska Lincoln, NB 68588	Nebraska Wesleyan University
New Mexico	University of New Mexico Albuquerque, NM 87131	University of Albuquerque
New York	Cornell University Ithaca, NY 14853	Ithaca College State University of New York—Cortland
	**New York State University Maritime College Fort Schuyler, Bronx, NY 10465	*Fordham University *Iona College *Manhattan College
	Rensselaer Polytechnic Institute Troy, NY 12180	Russell Sage College Siena College Skidmore College State University of New York—Albany Union College
	University of Rochester Rochester, NY 14627	Monroe Community College Nazareth College Rochester Institute of Technology St. John Fisher College State University of New York—Brockport State University of New York—Geneseo
North Carolina	Duke University Durham, NC 27706	North Carolina Central University
	University of North Carolina Chapel Hill, NC 27514	North Carolina State University
Ohio	Miami University Oxford, OH 45056	
	Ohio State University Columbus, OH 43210	Capital University Ohio Dominican College Otterbein College
Oklahoma	University of Oklahoma Norman, OK 73019	
Oregon	Oregon State University Corvallis, OR 97331	Linn Benton Community College
Pennsylvania	Pennsylvania State University University Park, PA 16802 (University Park campus only)	
	University of Pennsylvania Philadelphia, PA 19174	Drexel University LaSalle College St. Joseph's University Temple University
	Villanova University Villanova, PA 19085	Temple University

State	NROTC Unit	Crosstown Colleges/Universities
South Carolina	The Citadel Charleston, SC 29409 (Does not accept women)	
	University of South Carolina Columbia, SC 29208	
Tennessee	Memphis State University Memphis, TN 38111	
	Vanderbilt University Nashville, TN 37240	Belmont College David Lipscomb College Fisk University Tennessee State University Trevecca Nazarene College
Texas	Prairie View A&M University Prairie View, TX 77445	
	Rice University Houston, TX 77001	Houston Baptist University Texas Southern University University of Houston University of St. Thomas
	Texas A&M University College Station, TX 77843	
	Texas Tech University Lubbock, TX 79409	
	University of Texas Austin, TX 78712	
Utah	University of Utah Salt Lake City, UT 84112	Weber State College Westminster College
Vermont	Norwich University Northfield, VT 05663	
Virginia	Hampton Institute Hampton, VA 23668 Norfolk State University Norfolk, VA 23504 Old Dominion University Norfolk, VA 23508 (Consortium)	
	University of Virginia Charlottesville, VA 22903	
	Virginia Military Institute Lexington, VA 24450 (Does not accept women) Virginia Polytechnic Institute and State University Blacksburg, VA 24061	
Washington	University of Washington Seattle, WA 98195	Seattle Pacific University Seattle University
Wisconsin	Marquette University Milwaukee, WI 53233	*Milwaukee School of Engineering Mt. Mary College University of Wisconsin—Milwaukee
	University of Wisconsin Madison, WI 53706	

*Crosstown enrollment is pending formal agreement between the schools. May not be available during school year 1986.

**Marine Corps option not available

Index

military, 18, 19
 compulsory, 24
naval, 96
summer, 5, 46, 51, 58, 64, 68, 83,
 90, 99, 106
travel expenses, 1, 3, 5, 58, 62, 87,
 90, 92, 104
tuition, 1, 4, 31-32, 36, 39, 56, 62,
 69, 70, 82, 90

U
uniforms, 3, 4, 5, 19, 30, 58, 67, 82,
 83, 87, 90
Universal Military Training and
 Service Act, 24

V
Veterans Educational Assistance
 Program (VEAP), 71
Vietnam War, 21, 24, 25, 26, 27
Virginia Military Institute, 17

W
weapons systems, 12
women
 Air Force, 25, 58, 59
 Navy, 98, 106
 in ROTC, 27
 scholarships for, 25, 31
World War I, 19, 20
World War II, 21-22, 59